WAITING

for

WONDER

*Learning to Live on
God's Timeline*

MARLO
SCHALESKY

ABINGDON PRESS

NASHVILLE

WAITING FOR WONDER
LEARNING TO LIVE ON GOD'S TIMELINE

Copyright © 2016 by Marlo Schalesky

Library of Congress Cataloging-in-Publication Data

Names: Schalesky, Marlo M., 1967- author.
Title: Waiting for wonder : learning to live on God's timeline / Marlo Schalesky.
Description: Nashville : Abingdon Press, [2016] | Includes bibliographical references.
Identifiers: LCCN 2016011683 | ISBN 9781501820106 (pbk.)
Subjects: LCSH: Sarah (Biblical matriarch) | Expectation (Psychology)—Religious aspects—Christianity. | Trust in God—Christianity.
Classification: LCC BS580.S25 S33 2016 | DDC 222/.11092—dc23 LC record available at https://lccn.loc.gov/2016011683

16 17 18 19 20 21 22 23—10 9 8 7 6 5 4 3 2 1

MANUFACTURED IN THE UNITED STATES OF AMERICA

Mo

"Are you tired of waiting? Have you given up hope? Follow the journey of Sarah and make this book your traveling companion. With rich insights and refreshing hope, this powerful yet gentle gem will transform your weariness into wonder as you see with new eyes God's sacred and joyful purposes in your own wilderness of waiting. This book of encouragement is one you will turn to often and will want to share with your friends."

JUDY GORDON MORROW, author of *The Listening Heart*

"If you have ever felt forgotten, disappointed by life's outcomes or left wondering if you know how to hear God's voice, *Waiting for Wonder* is for you. Journeying with Sarah as she waits for God's promises to come to pass is heartrending and riveting. Marlo unveils, chapter by chapter, how hope springs up, even in your own life, when God is at work, hemming you in with wonder on every side."

SUSANNA FOTH AUGHTMON, author of *I Blame Eve, Breathing Through, A Trip Around the Sun,* and *Hope Sings*

"*Waiting for Wonder* by Marlo Schalesky touched my heart at a time when I was waiting for my own sense of wonder from the Lord. This book is one I could have highlighted sentence after sentence to refer back and remind myself of what is true. For instance, in one place she tells us that God is not thwarted by the actions of others and later hits home with 'sometimes what is happening is not all about you. Sometimes God is working a miracle in someone else.' I loved that because too often when life's trials hit home I want to make it personal. And while God may have a lesson for me in said trial, it's possible that He is using the trial for someone else—and I just happen to be in the way or part of the relationship—or even part of God's plan.

Waiting for Wonder is about hope. I have studied the life of Sarai/Sarah and found Schalesky's opinions to be very applicable and believable. She has taken an Old Testament story of heartache and struggle and forever waiting on God and turned it into a reason for us to trust Him with our lives today. If God wants *us* to wait as He did with Sarah, then maybe we need to learn some of the lessons she did. Engaging story. Well worth reading!"

JILL EILEEN SMITH, best-selling author of *The Crimson Cord* and *The Wives of King David* series.

"I started *Waiting for Wonder* with no concept of what I was in for—certainly not to be grabbed and held spellbound during the introduction—and not the tears that would well at the most inopportune times from that point forward. I sensed the Holy Spirit's hand in so many places along the way. I heard the voice of Jesus saying come closer, dig deeper, trust more fully. I plan to share this book with as many as will listen. It's truly a *must* read for every Christian."

MIRALEE FERRELL, best-selling, award-winning author of inspirational fiction

"In the drive-thru, E-Z, gotta-have-it-now world that is ours, waiting you'd think is a fat waste of time. Marlo Schalesky thinks otherwise, and her wisdom is soulful antidote, insightful balm. In plainspoken poetry she probes the not-oft-explored landscape: the hollow canyons of our souls, the barrenness that leaves us aching, gasping, teetering at the precipice of doubt and despair. Schalesky is a writer whose hard-won courage makes her a truth-teller we can lean on, those of us who know barrenness in its varied iterations. She writes us into hope. And along the way illuminates the pure wonder of waiting."

BARBARA MAHANY, author of *Slowing Time*

"No one can experience this book and not be moved—or changed. This is required reading for any Christian who wants to understand the God whose ways are not our ways and trust Him still."

DR. REBECCA PRICE JANNEY, author of 19 books, historian, speaker

"Can a book calm you and stimulate you simultaneously? *Waiting for Wonder* settles the angst of the modern soul long enough to carve out a quiet space where a reader can receive the challenge to follow Jesus deeper. Schalesky's words quietly slipped into my soul where God used them to wedge loose rock-hard places to make room for transformation and life. The writer did my favorite thing: respecting biblical characters as the human beings they were, she sifted through their stories for the truth that remains transformative for the modern soul and delivered this truth with humility and grace. I can't wait to read it again."

LORI STANLEY ROELEVELD, author of *Jesus and the Beanstalk*

"*Waiting for Wonder* doesn't merely reveal Marlo Schalesky's elegance with language, devotion to the unfailing truth of God's Word, and her ability to discover wonder-filled moments. The book does what all good books should: it invites us to think. And in the thinking and pondering, our hearts are opened to how God infuses breathless wonder in our waiting."

CYNTHIA RUCHTI, speaker and author of *Ragged Hope* and *Tattered and Mended*

To Joelle
who knows how to wait well

*The L*ORD *is good to those who wait for Him,*
To the soul who seeks Him.
It is good that one should hope and wait quietly
*For the salvation of the L*ORD.

—Lamentations 3:25-26 (NKJV)

Contents

INTRODUCTION

I will make of you a great nation and will bless you. I will make your name respected, and you will be a blessing.
> *I will bless those who bless you,*
> *those who curse you I will curse;*
> *all the families of the earth*
> *will be blessed because of you.*

—Genesis 12:2-3

I COME TO SARAH'S LIFE RELUCTANTLY, my head turned, my eyes cast down. My heart shrinks from this life filled with decades of promises still not come true, of desperate prayers that hang and shimmer and groan through months turned to years. I ache with the hope of a whole world blessed and tremor as I wrestle with the wonder of waiting.

Sarah's waiting. And my own.

This life she lived millennia ago is too much like mine. Her God too much like the one I follow. And my soul whispers, pants, and dares to ask, "Who is this God?"

Who is he who makes impossible promises then asks us to wait? Who is he who shows us the stars in the sky when we don't see even a glimmer of hope? Who is he, when months turn to years and stretch to decades, and still we wait? Who is this God of long intervals, painful delays, and yet-unanswered prayer?

Is he the God of waiting?

I ponder the question as I stand in my barn, shovel in my hand. I scoop another load of horse manure. I put it in the muck bucket. Just like yesterday, and the day before, the week before, the year before. Just like tomorrow and the day after that. I scoop and nothing changes. I hope and still must shovel.

This is not my dream. I had bold and beautiful dreams. When I was fifteen, God told me if I wanted to change the world, I must follow him. I followed. Yet, here I am decades later, shovel in hand, ankle-deep in stink. God's timing is so rarely my own.

For a moment, I pause and let the shovel fall. I stare out over the pasture. Fog lies like an ashen blanket over the trees, the grass, the once-white fences. It hides the beauty. It smothers my sight of things beyond. And I remember that fifteen-year-old girl. She was so full of hope and promise and vision. She believed that all she had to do to succeed, to make a difference in the world, was follow God and believe. She didn't see obstacles. She didn't anticipate waiting. She had no doubts.

But I have doubts.

And vision is covered by the pressing grayness.

I sense the weight of the fog, the dampness, the work, and the manure in the depths of my soul. Is this all life is? Scooping poop in the dreary mist? Where are the promises? Where is the dream of a life that will make a difference in this world? Where is God in the fog, the wet, and the shoveling of stink?

It's easy to believe God when a promise is new and fresh, bubbling with life. It's hard when the years pass and nothing changes. It's hard to keep praying, keep hoping, keep believing. It's hard when those you love betray you, when desperation strikes, when your own plans backfire, and still God does not fill the emptiness.

I close my eyes and take up the shovel again, knowing that if I am to find God, if I am to grasp his wonder, I must find him here. I must trust him in the in-between places. I must discover the wonder of fog and horse manure—the wonder of waiting.

I want to find him anew, this God of the waiting room, find him where he seems most absent. I want to know this God who asks "Is anything too difficult for the Lord?" and brings laughter when it seems too late.

I need Sarah to lead me there. I long to place my hand in hers and whisper, "Let me see him as you did. Reveal to me this God of wonder-while-you-wait." And perhaps, if I see him as she did, the whole world will indeed be blessed. But for this moment, I need her to show me a God who is determined, breathtaking, and beyond all my plans.

Maybe you do, too.

Come, walk with me through Sarah's life. Embark on this journey through disappointment, doubt, and detours to discover God in the "not yet" places of life. Believe again in his tireless commitment to "bless all the families of the earth" through you. He is calling you, as he called her, to wonder, to laughter in the face of the impossible, to a blessing not just for you but for the whole world.

Come, discover this God of waiting, of stars in a silent sky, of fog and shovels and a whole world blessed. Breathe deeply of the wonder of waiting.

1

WHO ARE YOU? IDENTITY AND SHAME

Abram's wife was Sarai. . . . Sarai was unable to have children.

—Genesis 11:29-30

*B*ARREN. A HARSH WORD, unkind, unyielding. I shiver and wonder if there was not a gentler way to introduce this woman through whom the whole world would be blessed. The Common English Bible shares my sentiment and softens the blow with "Sarai was unable to have children." The original Hebrew, however, is much less kind: "Sarai was barren. There is no child to her" (my translation).

Why, Lord, why must this be the introduction to Sarai, Abram's beloved wife?

Not beautiful Sarai.

Not faithful Sarai.

Not strong, determined, hopeful Sarai.

Barren Sarai.

Must we really start there?

Somehow, yes. We must begin with the lack, the shame, the hopelessness. We must first accept the barrenness if we are to continue on the journey to the place God promises.

So I grapple with that barrenness. And I see that there are barren places in us all. We have spots hidden away in our souls that are without life, where hope has shriveled and all we want to do is cringe and deny the dryness. There are places of doubt, of despair, of weakness, of shame, of guilt and pain.

We are all barren.

And Sarai gives us hope.

So I'm glad the Bible does not shy away from Sarai's shame. I'm glad it starts with this almost cruel introduction. I'm glad because it tells me that Sarai's journey can be my own. God sees my barrenness and meets it with promise—meets me in the very place where I have the least hope, the most pain, the most shame.

Do I dare embrace my barrenness? Do I dare acknowledge my shame? And in doing so, might I embrace the very promises of God?

For Sarai, it might have felt something like this.

Sarai Tells Her Story

I never dreamed my shame would define me. I never imagined I would be known for the very thing that causes me the deepest pain.

Everyone I know has children. Everyone but me. Decades have passed. Hope has turned to a bitter herb in my mouth. Dust stirs around me as I make my way to the marketplace of Ur. They know me here, know that I am barren, childless. And they whisper.

Today, as always, the marketplace buzzes with the sounds of children's laughter, the murmuring gossip of women, the shouts of merchants. And beyond that, I hear the footfalls of worshipers traveling to the great ziggurat, the temple tower, just built by King Ur-Nammu. Its bricks rise over the city, calling us to the worship of Nanna, the moon god. Calling me to come and beg favor from a god of fertility.

I do not listen.

I will not go.

Instead, I pause beside a cloth-maker's booth. I block out the sounds of the children, the mothers, and the silent beckoning from the temple of Ur. I stare at the bolts of cloth. A deep red, a tired yellow, a pale blue. My fingers barely brush the rough weave. The blue cloth would make a good garment for travel.

Travel? Why do I think of these things? Perhaps because the walls of the city seem to press in on me today, the dust, the noise, the thousand voices, the footsteps, and the temple. Mostly the temple. And the children. And the whispers that always follow me.

The pitying glances.

The cruel conjectures.

The snide advice that always involves a trip to a tower of bricks timed with the moon's transformations.

Barren Sarai. Childless Sarai. The one whom the gods hate.

Shame. Guilt. Pain.

Hopelessness. Helplessness. Despair.

I choose the bolt of blue cloth. My fingers fumble as I pay. Blue cloth. For travel. But where would I ever go?

"Sarai."

I hear my name spoken gently. I hear it despite the bustle of the city all around me.

"Sarai."

I turn. He is there, my Abram, standing behind me. He has come from tending his sheep. It is too early for him to come in.

He moves closer, his hand touching my arm. "Follow me, we must speak." He takes the cloth from me, and my hand flutters to my belly, flat as always.

The noises fade as we walk out from the shadow of the great temple. We walk toward home. Then my Abram speaks.

"*Elohim* has spoken to me. God, our Creator, has come to me."

"You saw him?"

"No one sees him and lives. But he spoke to me all the same." Abram's voice catches, lowers. "He made us a promise. An impossible promise."

My hand drops to my belly again.

Abram pauses, swallows, and I see the wonder in his eyes. "He has told me to leave here, go from our father's house, to a land he will show me."

"Leave?" A blue cloth, just right for a garment for travel.

"And, and . . . he has promised to make me into a great nation."

My hand falls. My heart constricts. What kind of promise is this? I am barren. Decades barren. Who is this God who promises a nation? Who is this *Elohim* who makes promises in the place of my deepest pain?

"Listen, Sarai. He says we are chosen, and all the peoples on earth will be blessed through us."

Us? How could it be us? I tremble and straighten my shoulders. I fight to hide my tears.

But he sees them anyway.

And there, with the cries of children playing in the distance, with the soft tread of feet toward a temple to the city's god, with a blue cloth for travel, I weep and wonder.

Does this God of promise see me after all? Does he know who I am?

I draw a long breath. "When?"

"I don't know. He said only what I've told you already. But this I know." My husband's eyes search mine. "The promise is for us, Sarai. *Elohim*, God himself, will accomplish it."

I press my lips tightly shut. Isn't it already too late? This *Elohim* could have promised wealth, power, beauty, long life. But instead he promises to remove my shame.

What kind of crazy, impossible promise is this? No one calls a barren woman to birth a great nation. No one chooses the childless to bless the whole world through her seed. No one but Abram's God would do such a thing.

No one but *Elohim* would dare.

Waiting for Wonder

What would it be like, I wonder, to be described by the very thing that brings you the most shame, the most pain, the most guilt?

"This is my friend, Ann. She screams at her kids."

"This is Tony. He's an ex-con. He killed someone."

"Meet Sue, she gossips."

"Here's Jose, who can't keep a job."

"Amy, failed marriage."

"Ted, out-of-control rages."

"Lisa, molested as a child."

"John, adulterer."

"Maria, quitter."

"Bob, drug addict."

"Rachel, bigot."

"John, attempted suicide."

Sarai, infertile. She has no children.

I don't want to be identified by my failures. I don't want the first thing people know about me to be the very thing I most wish to hide. But that's how the Bible chooses to introduce Sarai. It labels her "barren," then adds "no child" to underscore her pain. The biblical description is stark, harsh.

Why does the Bible introduce her this way?

Expectations

In Sarai's day, the primary role of women was to produce children, particularly an heir. A wife's value to her husband as well as to society was directly attached to the number of her sons. The main purpose of marriage was to procreate, and children were seen as direct proof of blessing from the gods. In Abram and Sarai's faith, the idea of children as a sign of God's blessing came directly from his words to Adam and Eve recorded in Genesis 1:28: "God blessed them and said to them, 'Be fertile and multiply; fill the earth and master it.'" The blessing of children is confirmed again in Genesis 9:7 when God blessed Noah and his sons after the flood, saying, "As for you, be fertile and multiply. Populate the earth and multiply in it." In both Genesis 1 and 9, the blessing is coupled with a command to procreate.

The inability to do so was a source of not only disappointment for the ancient woman but also great shame. She could not perform her duty or call. She was without worth. Sometimes, if a man could afford it, a second wife could be taken to provide children and the infertile wife could be retained. But divorce was considered a viable option for the husband of an infertile wife. In Egypt it appears that the marriage was not even considered complete until childbirth, and the woman could be put aside at any time without a formal divorce.[1]

In Sarai's day and throughout the Old Testament, infertile women were despised, rejected, helpless, and considered cursed.

Given the reproach and societal shame of barrenness, it becomes even more poignant that Sarai is introduced in this way. Commentator John Walton emphasizes this view, saying, "We find out that Abram's wife, Sarai, is barren, leaving the uninformed reader every reason to dismiss that line of the family."[2]

But God does not dismiss them. Instead, he specifically calls them to be what they are least likely to be. He calls the childless, the infertile, the barren to birth a nation through whom the whole world will be blessed. The place in her life that causes the most shame, pain, and hopelessness for Sarai is exactly the place where God makes his wildest, most impossible promises. It's the very place he chooses to work.

I've seen this kind of thing from God before.

Reversals

She sits across from me at Denny's, this mother of a murderer. Tears fill her eyes. Her hands shake just a little. She bears a label that should cause shame. It does cause pain. She who could not save her own son. She who lives with the reality of loss every day. I stab my eggs with a fork. She stabs my soul with a story.

Her story, so unlike Sarai's yet so like it, too.

She speaks of a mother's worst nightmare. She speaks of a son addicted to drugs, of a broken marriage, of grandchildren far away, of broken hearts and broken dreams. She tells of prayers and weeping, of a son's suicide attempt and the institution that followed. She speaks with a pain so deep that I lower my fork, my eggs forgotten.

And then her voice softens. I hear of murder and a son's reckless escape. Arrest, imprisonment, seeking, and hurt. I hear from a mother whose son never left prison. He died there of blood cancer.

She is the mother of a murderer.

She is the mother of a dead son.

She is my friend.

And her life and ministry are filled with beauty and promise I have rarely seen. I know of her passion to reach other men in prison with the love and good news of Jesus. I know how she hugs the unhuggable and brings hope to the hopeless. I know of the men whose lives have changed because they have encountered Christ through her and come to know him for themselves. I know of a young man who is now living with her after his release, a man sporting gang tattoos and a horrific past. But this young man is now focused on saving others from gang life. He would love to have his tattoos removed, but God is using them to reach those whom others can't reach. God is using the marks of his shame, making them into signs of God's purposes.

So I see a pattern of transforming our shame. It is the pattern of Sarai.

I ponder the pattern as this mother tells me what breaks her heart. It is not what I expect. "For me, it is the incarcerated who are doing life without knowing our Lord. Also the ones who have found him after incarceration and their families who have to do life without them. God has taught me so much with having this in my family. My eyes have been opened to so much more than what I would have known. So I thank God for opening my heart so wide."

It is out of a broken heart that God's glory shines. So I must ask her again about this ministry to inmates and their families. I must ask her how she can go into the prisons, encounter her own pain, day after day, week after week, year after year. Why does she bring hugs and the hope of Jesus? How can she, especially in the light of her son's recent death?

She looks at me then with those tear-stained eyes across a table filled with bacon and eggs, toast and fruit. She looks at me and I see these are not tears of despair but of a deep, indescribable joy. It takes my breath away.

Then she says something so simple, so profound that I stop to savor it. She says, "Because their pain is my pain, you know."

And I see. For a moment, I see God's truth so clearly: he is the God who calls us at the very place of our deepest shame, our deepest pain, and transforms that place into something with breathtaking beauty. No one but God—no one but *Elohim*—would dare do such a thing.

So I look across that table at Denny's and I see the heart of God in the eyes of a dead murderer's mother. I see pain so deep that it has been transformed to glory by the only One who can reach those places in our soul. I see an impossible promise come true. I see the God who calls a barren woman to birth a nation of promise.

I see hope.

God's Specialty

Old Testament scholar Walter Brueggemann calls barrenness in Sarai's time "an effective metaphor for hopelessness . . . no human power to invent a future."[3] To strengthen the point, the Bible chooses to set Sarai's barrenness against the backdrop of her husband's family's fertility. Just a few verses before her introduction, the Genesis account outlines the genealogy of her husband's ancestor Shem, with his grandfather, Nahor, the youngest to become a parent at twenty-nine years old. Later, we read that Abram's brother, also named Nahor, had eight sons by his wife, Milcah, and four more sons through his concubine Reumah (Genesis 22:23-24).

But Sarai was barren. There were no children to her. *The New American Commentary* notes, "Not only at this point does Sarai have no beginnings, she also has no continuation through a child. The message is thunderous: the woman is a 'weak link,' we would say, in the chain of blessing. Her barren state dominates the Abraham story since the divine promises involve a numerous host of progeny for Abraham."[4]

But God chose Abram, and he chose Sarai, anyway. Nowhere does the text imply that Abram's marriage to Sarai was a mistake. Her barrenness wasn't something God reluctantly had to overcome. Neither did Sarai earn the promises of descendants, land, and a whole-world blessing through extra faithfulness, goodness, or devotion. We know this precisely because the Genesis account introduces her by her barrenness. It says nothing else about her. It only emphasizes her lack, her shame, what she does not have and cannot do. It refuses to soften or shirk away from her barrenness. Instead it confronts it, overcomes it.

The biblical account affirms that God looks barrenness in the face and makes his promises anyway. Or perhaps it would be more accurate to say he promises *because*. From the beginning of Sarai's "chosenness," God chose the impossible, he chose to transform, and he chose the redemption of her shame and ours. He did not call a fertile woman to birth a nation. He chose a barren one—on purpose.

"Despite her dim prospects, Sarai emerges by God's gracious intervention to achieve the regal stature that her name 'princess' conveys. She becomes the matriarch of all Israel (Isa 51:2)," says scholar Kenneth Mathews.[5]

And that tells us that God's delight has always been the full, true, complete redemption of the things in our lives that we hate the most, the things that cause the deepest sorrow, the worst guilt, the most agonizing pain. Those are the very things God longs to transform—for Sarai and for us.

Not because we've earned it or done enough to make up for it.

Not because we've hidden it or done a good job covering it up with other good deeds.

Not because we're beautiful or deserving or extra-faithful.

But because somehow this is his purpose. His specialty.

It is who he is.

Who Is This God?

So I wrestle with this vision of a God who allows a woman to suffer barrenness for decades. I ask him why she had to be infertile at all. And I think of a man born blind, a man who could do nothing but beg, could not enter the temple, could not make sacrifices, could not draw close to God in the way that his culture dictated. For decades.

His story is found in John 9. Jesus came upon the blind man. His disciples asked, "Rabbi, who sinned so that he was born blind, this man or his parents?" (v. 2). Surely something as terrible as blindness was caused by someone's sin! But Jesus didn't answer in the way his disciples expected, or as we expect. Instead he said, "Neither he nor his parents. This happened so that God's mighty works might be displayed in him" (v. 3). Blindness was meant to reveal the glory of God. He had suffered for his entire life, and then God took the very thing that caused him the most pain and transformed it to bless not only him but us as well. Millennia later, we still hear the testimony of the man born blind. We are blessed. God is glorified.

And then I think of a Samaritan woman going to a well to draw water at midday, a woman so filled with shame that she did not go to the well in the morning with the other women. Jesus met her there, at the place that epitomized her shame. They spoke of Jacob's well and living water, but none of that changed her. Rather it took Jesus' confronting her shame, revealing that which she wanted to keep hidden, to transform this woman from avoider to missionary. John 4 tells us the story:

> Jesus said to her, "Go, get your husband, and come back here." The woman replied, "I don't have a husband." "You are right to say, 'I don't have a husband,'" Jesus answered. "You've had five husbands,

and the man you are with now isn't your husband. You've spoken the truth." (vv. 16-18)

As in Genesis's introduction of Sarai, Jesus confronted, without apology, the shame and pain a woman wanted to keep hidden. And this became the exact thing that blessed the others in her village. Verses 28-30 tell us, "The woman put down her water jar and went into the city. She said to the people, 'Come and see a man who has told me everything I've done! Could this man be the Christ?' They left the city and were on their way to see Jesus."

The Samaritan woman went to the well at midday to hide her shame from others. But then that became the very thing she used to bring the townspeople to Jesus. She didn't say, "Here is someone promising living water," or "Here is someone explaining theology." Instead she proclaimed, "Here is someone who revealed my deepest shame and made promises anyway. Could this man be the Messiah?"

He could, because that is who God is.

This is a God who promises descendants as numerous as the grains of sand to a barren woman.

This is a God who blesses all the families on earth through a woman with no family at all.

He is a God who reveals his glory through an outcast—a man born blind, who could not enter the temple.

And he reaches an entire town through a woman so ashamed she went to a well in the middle of the day.

This is what God does. God chooses us precisely for the places where nothing seems to change and hope is sparse. He is the God who uncovers the deepest places of our shame and pain and promises to bless the whole world right from those very places.

We sit in our barrenness, in our blindness, in our shame. We may sit for a long time. But we do not sit without hope. Like Sarai, we hold the strange, impossible promises of God.

So I look at Sarai and I see my own barrenness. I ask myself: will I set forth on this journey with her to discover a God who promises to transform me to bless the whole world?

Will I dare step forward knowing that the agonies of my soul will be revealed, my pain will have no secrets, and his promises may take decades to be fulfilled?

Do I dare embrace the barrenness and submit to the power of waiting, to the power and promises of *Elohim* himself?

I will dare. Will you?

> *Look! I'm doing a new thing;*
>   *now it sprouts up; don't you recognize it?*
> *I'm making a way in the desert,*
>   *paths in the wilderness.*

> —Isaiah 43:19

2

STUCK IN-BETWEEN: SETTLING IN HARAN

Terah took his son Abram, his grandson Lot (son of Haran), and his son Abram's wife, Sarai his daughter-in-law. They left Ur of the Chaldeans for the land of Canaan, and arriving at Haran, they settled there.

—Genesis 11:31

HALFWAY FROM EVERYTHING THEY knew. Halfway to everything they'd been promised. Stuck. Waiting. Can't go forward, can't go back. Trapped.

Already I don't like the story. Already my brows furrow, my lips purse. I want to read that Abram took Sarai and they traveled directly to the promised land. Acts 7:2-4 tells us that Abram received God's call while he was still in Ur, before he settled in Haran. I want to believe that when God calls, the journey will be straight, unhindered, and without delays. There will be no stuck-halfway, no settling in the in-between place where the past is behind yet the promises of God still seem distant.

But I don't always get what I want. In Sarai's story, or in my own.

For us both, there is Haran.

I don't like Haran.

Perhaps Sarai didn't either. Perhaps her struggles are our struggles, her questions echo our own.

Who is the God of promise when you've settled in a place you don't want to be and the power to move on is not in your hands? How do you live with hope, with faith, when stuck in-between? How do you wait, believe, and hang on to the promises when you're living in Haran?

Perhaps for Sarai it happened something like this.

Sarai Tells Her Story

*H*aran. It's too much like a smaller version of Ur. There are merchants, music, streets lined with stone. People worship the same moon god we left behind. We traveled for days, weeks. We trudged through heat and cold, dust and dryness. We walked until our backs ached and our feet blistered. We traveled on hope and promise. Five hundred miles, maybe six. Long days, short nights.

And here we are. Haran.

It is a fertile land, well-watered. Safe. But this is not the place we were promised.

Worshipers head to the temple of Nanna. My husband's father, Terah, goes with them. I wander the marketplace. The voices of children buzz through the air. Women gossip. Old men shout. A merchant sells blue cloth.

Blue cloth.

Mine is worn and tattered now. It is gray. And I am gray. Gray with hope forestalled. With the dust of delayed dreams. Gray with promises unfulfilled.

I am gray with waiting.

There is no child, no new land. Nothing but this in-between place that is too like everything I hoped to leave behind.

We were promised so much more.

Terah will not move on. We cannot convince him. He has settled here. So we settle, too. Abram tends sheep. Lot haggles for goods we do not need. And Terah travels to the temple to pray to a moon god who will not give him the grandson he longs for.

We settle . . . for so much less than I dreamed.

I love my husband's father. I love my husband. But I do not love Haran. Will I ever leave here? Will I ever see the land of promise?

I look at the new blue cloth the vendor holds. I do not touch it. I cannot. Because the power to change lies outside myself. I can only wait, and wonder.

Where is the God who called us to so much more? Does he see me even on the streets of Haran? Does he remember that this is not where we belong?

I do not want to stay here forever.

I die a little in the waiting.

And I wonder, does something else need to die before I can move from the place of in-between?

Waiting for Wonder

It's a chilling question. What has to die before we can get unstuck, before we can continue toward the promise of God?

The Bible doesn't tell us what Abram and Sarai thought of settling in Haran. Nor does it give explanations as to why they settled there.

Archaeology tells us much about both Ur, where they came from, and Haran, where they settled. In Abram's time, approximately a quarter million people lived in Ur. Homes were often two to three stories high and built around comfortable courtyards. Musical instruments and jewelry were plentiful. The culture was advanced in math and architecture, as evidenced by the great ziggurat, or massive stepped tower, upon which sat the temple of the moon god, Nanna, who was associated with giving fertility, divining the future, and determining destinies. The ziggurat and temple, built by King Ur-Nammu, dominated the city. An archeological dig led by Sir Leonard Woolley in the 1920s also revealed evidence of human sacrifice in the royal tomb in Ur.[1]

Similarly, Haran was also a central city for the worship of the moon god. Located on the bank of the Balikh River, nearly six hundred miles northwest of Ur, it was fertile, well-watered, and an important city of trade in the ancient world.[2] For Sarai, Haran would have been very similar to the great city she had left behind.

So why did the family stop short of the promise? They had not set out planning on a long stay in Haran. Did they get discouraged by the long journey? Were they weary? Were the luxuries of Haran too tempting? Or Terah too frail? Was settling for less than the promise easier than pushing on? We don't know.

21

But we do know that Haran was not just a quick stop at the local roadside motel. It was not a few weeks or months in a rental for travelers. No, they got stuck. Sarai got stuck. In the waiting place.

Sometimes we do, too.

The Waiting Place

Waiting. I've never been a fan. But it seems I have a PhD in the art. Waiting for the results of infertility treatments, waiting for an offer for a job, waiting for a change in a relationship, waiting for a change in life.

And recently, waiting for test results that could mean cancer or mean nothing. Once again, I was in the waiting place. I was stuck in Haran. And while there, I wrote this:

> I find myself here again, in this waiting place. The place where I know God is sovereign. I know he holds my life in his hands. I know he is there. I know he cares. I know the very hairs on my head are numbered . . . as are my days.
>
> And yet there is a knot in my stomach and my eyes flicker to the phone. Again. And again. It does not ring. Not yet. Of course not yet.
>
> But I watch anyway. I swallow. And remind myself of all the things I already know.

- Who among you by worrying can add a single moment to your life? (Matthew 6:27 and Luke 12:25)
- Therefore, stop worrying about tomorrow, because tomorrow will worry about itself. (Matthew 6:34)
- Therefore, I say to you, don't worry about your life. (Luke 12:22)
- Don't be anxious about anything. (Philippians 4:6)

And my glance skitters to the phone again.

Today I had my yearly mammogram and screening. Today they found something on my right side. Today could be the first day of a very painful journey.

But I don't know yet. I am stuck here, in-between.

It's the not knowing that twists through my soul. It's the not being able to move forward. Not being able to move back. Trust is harder in the waiting place.

So I watch the phone even though I know the radiologist probably hasn't even looked at the scans. Even though I know it is too soon. Even though, if she calls, it will only be to bring me in for more tests.

I hate waiting.

But it's not a choice.

It's something that's thrust upon you.

And still I wait. . . . I drown in the waiting.

God, you were with me in the past. You will be with me no matter the future.

Are you here, too, in the waiting place?

The test results came back as benign. But even if they had not, I've found that waiting is often the hardest part of a journey because we feel a unique kind of fear, of dread in the waiting place. We sense that nothing is in our control. We cannot just "do something." We can't fix it. There is no plan to foster hope, no to-do list to get us out. We don't know when change will come, and deep inside we carry the fear that we may be stuck forever in the awkward, painful in-between of Haran.

I have a friend who is getting divorced. For two years she's been in proceedings and nothing is yet settled. "Divorce is awful," she says. "But the waiting to get divorced is even worse. I can't make plans. I can't move on. I can't even start to heal."

That is the struggle of the waiting place. It is the fight against fear, against despair. It is the fight to remember the promises of God when they aren't getting any nearer.

Who's in Charge?

When we're feeling stuck in the waiting place, our culture says, "Get out of that rut! Life's too short. Stop the excuses. Do something." In *The Huffington Post*, you can find thirteen inspirational quotes for when you're stuck in a rut. You'll be told to smile more, care less, be happy, and think good thoughts.[3] Elsewhere, you might find thirty quotes that will "most certainly get you out of any rut," where you can read that you need to rise up and attack your day, and never give up.[4]

Good advice, but sometimes change is outside our control. Sometimes we're not in charge. Sometimes we're stuck in Haran and something must die before we can move forward.

Something must change, and only God himself can accomplish what needs to be done.

Our text underscores Terah's authority over his family when settling in Haran. It says, "Terah took his son Abram . . . and his son Abram's wife, Sarai" (Genesis 11:31). Sarai cannot choose to continue the journey. God must remove a barrier before she can move forward.

In this case, Terah himself must die.

What Has to Die?

What is God doing while you're stuck in Haran? Does the wait have purpose? Yes!

We know little about Abram's father, Terah. Besides his lineage and age, we know he did not worship the God of Israel. Joshua told the Israelites, "Long ago your ancestors lived on the other side of the Euphrates. They served other gods. Among them was Terah the father of Abraham and Nahor" (Joshua 24:2).

Terah did not worship the God of Abram and Sarai. Most likely he worshiped Nanna, both in Ur and Haran. So, idolatry followed Sarai to Haran and settled with her there.

Only when God himself removed idolatry through the death of Terah could Sarai and Abram move on toward the promises of God. As expressed by Old Testament scholar Bruce Waltke, "Terah himself will die, having settled for a land short of Abraham's heavenly vision."[5]

Sometimes there are idols in our lives too, idols we cannot remove on our own. Sometimes we don't even know they're there. Sometimes they are bound up in those we love. Sometimes we're bound up in relationships from which only God can free us. We fret, we squirm, we question, we wait, not knowing why we must.

But in the wait, God is doing a work. He is making himself the only God in our lives. That is the lesson of Haran. The waiting place has purpose. God is doing his work there, in his timing, not ours.

God often makes me wait in Haran. And as I look at Sarai and ponder Terah's worship of the moon god, I see that my God wants to cleanse me of Nanna worship as well. Nanna was a god of fertility. God wants me to trust him for my family. People sought Nanna to divine the future. God wants me to trust my future in his hands, without needing to know what the next days, weeks, months, or years hold. Nanna was supposed to determine one's destiny. God wants to fulfill my destiny as I simply follow him with faith and obedience.

My need for security, to know what will happen, and even to make a difference in the world must all die with Terah. As I wait in faith, God is preparing me for the rest of the journey. He is preparing me for the promise.

I still hate the waiting place. But as I look at Sarai, as I look at my life, I see that God is at work in the waiting place. Not one moment falls to the ground in vain. Never in the rest of Sarai's story do we hear of her or anyone with her worshiping another god. Even when she became desperate, even when she tried to force the promise of a son through a means God did not provide, even when it looked as if there was no hope at all, she did not turn to a fertility god. Sarai worshiped neither Nanna nor the gods of Canaan. She refused to reject the God of her husband, Abram.

With Terah's death in Haran, their household, their family, was cleansed of idolatry. And I wonder, in all our lives, if that is the purpose of the waiting place. God is doing a forever-work that will knit our hearts to his. We can't always see it; we rarely understand it. But God is working with power and wonder and might to make us more fully his own.

In our lives, and in Sarai's, Haran is an essential part of the journey. God does a deep work there, a work we could never do ourselves.

Catching a Glimpse of God

If God's purpose is to become our only God in the waiting place, what are we to do as we wait? As we stare at the phone waiting for a call from the doctor's office, as we watch out the window for the mail truck bringing good or bad news, as we wait for a job offer, a reconciliation, a change in family, in health, in home. . . . As we find ourselves halfway between the old life and the promise of the new, as we squirm in the stuck places of life, how do we live? How do we live with confidence and faith and joy? How do we live in the wonder of God?

It's a question I've long wrestled with, but a few years ago my baby boy gave me a glimpse of what it means to live in the fullness of God in the waiting places of life.

I finished feeding him, then plopped him into his playpen with his toys. Next I went about doing all the things I had to do: dishes and laundry, bills and hair brushing, preparing a snack, cleaning the kitchen, picking up toys, making beds, rubbing antibiotic ointment on a variety of owies, picking up more toys, and preparing a safe place for Jayden to play and grow and learn how to crawl.

Meanwhile, Jayden chewed his rubber ducky, rattled his toy rattle, squeaked his bear, and pushed the button to make his stuffed dog sing the ABC song. As I passed by his playpen once, twice, three times, I began to notice something. Every time he caught a glimpse of me, he looked up, grinned, clapped his hands, and raised his arms.

The third time he did it I had to stop because something about his actions reminded me of worship, of clapping to a song, of raising my hands in praise.

Baby Jayden was in his little playpen world, busy with his playpen toys, waiting for the freedom of the promised land outside the confines of that same playpen. And yet, even as he waited he was watching too, eager for a glimpse of the one who loved him, who was preparing the way for his growth, and who knew the right time to lift him out.

As I paused and picked him up, he laughed and clapped his hands some more. That was when I knew I needed to be a lot more

27

like him. Instead of fretting in the playpens of life, I needed to keep watch for the One who provides, prepares, and loves. I needed to keep an eye out for God working around me and in me. If I wanted to be as happy as baby Jayden, I needed to put myself in a position to see God's glory whenever he passed by. I needed to be like Moses in Exodus 33:21-23: "The LORD said, 'Here is a place near me where you will stand beside the rock. As my glorious presence passes by, I'll set you in a gap in the rock, and I'll cover you with my hand until I've passed by. Then I'll take away my hand, and you will see my back.'"

All Moses wanted was God's presence, a glimpse of his glory. And God put him in the cleft of a rock, in a playpen, in the waiting place. In Haran. All Moses had to do was watch. All Jayden did was watch. And I wonder, did Sarai watch too? Did she watch for God to move?

Genesis 11:32 states, "Terah lived 205 years, and he died in Haran." Chapter 12 opens with the renewal of the promise to Abram.

When we wait in faith, when we watch for God in the in-between of Haran, he will renew his promises as soon as the purposes of the waiting place are complete. We will not wait forever. We do not wait in vain.

God will call us from Haran. Wait, watch, and glimpse his glory.

Who Is This God?

Who is this God who sometimes doesn't move fast enough? Who is he who allows us to be stuck in Haran for months, even years? Who plops us in the playpen when we want to be free to pursue life's promises?

He is the God of Sarai. He is the God of Haran.

Just as he was the God who called a man to build an ark when there was no raincloud in the sky. For years, Noah labored in the place between a promise and its fulfillment. He kept faith in the dry place because God had promised a flood. And it was in the dryness that he became a man of faith. Hebrews 11:7 tells us, "By faith Noah responded with godly fear when he was warned about events he hadn't seen yet. He built an ark to deliver his household. With his faith, he criticized the world and became an heir of the righteousness that comes from faith." He didn't become a man of faith in the ark; he became one in the dry in-between place. God is the God of the dry places.

He is the God who anointed a man named David to be king of Israel but did not give him the throne for years to come. First, David was a fugitive and an exile chased by King Saul, who desired his death. Even after Saul died, David did not reign from Jerusalem. Instead God placed him in Hebron, where he reigned over Judah for seven and a half years before he became king over all Israel (2 Samuel 1–5). God was working in David's exile. God was working in Hebron. There David became a man after God's own heart. Acts 13:22 tells us, "After God removed him [Saul], he raised up David to be their king. God testified concerning him, 'I have found David, Jesse's son, a man who shares my desires. Whatever my will is, he will do.'" It was in Hebron, the in-between place, that God purified a king's heart. God is the God of Hebron.

He is the God who waited in the wilderness for forty days and forty nights, tested by Satan, before beginning his ministry (Mark 1:9-13). In the in-between of the wilderness, even Jesus needed to be prepared for the promise that would save us all. Even Jesus waited in the in-between. God is the God of the wilderness.

He is the God who healed a man halfway, so people appeared as trees walking. Afterward he healed him fully (Mark 8:22-25). God is the God of the halfway point. Halfway wasn't a mistake. It wasn't a failure. It was the platform to perform something more. It was the gateway to wonder.

He is the God who told his own mother, who had been waiting for the fulfillment of the promises given her since his conception, "My time hasn't come yet" (John 2:4). Mary waited thirty years for her son's ministry to begin. God is the God of the long wait.

And He is the God who goes to prepare a place for us because everything in this life is Haran. We live in the in-between place every day. We have not arrived at the promise of eternal life. We live every single day of our lives in the "not yet."

And in this in-between, halfway-to-heaven place, Jesus tells us: "Don't be troubled. Trust in God. Trust also in me. My Father's house has room to spare. If that weren't the case, would I have told you that I'm going to prepare a place for you? When I go to prepare a place for you, I will return and take you to be with me so that where I am you will be too" (John 14:1-3).

So in the wait we remember that where we are now is not all we've been promised. This life is not the promised land. We live in Haran, halfway from where we've been and to where God has promised. God is with us. God is working. There is purpose in the waiting place.

Do not let your heart be troubled. Look for glimpses of him. When waiting for the phone call, when you don't know what will happen next, when all you feel is stuck where you never wanted to be, he is freeing you to love him fully. He is doing the work. He is preparing the way.

He will take you toward the promises when the time is right. Watch for him. Trust. And catch a glimpse of his glory, even in Haran.

> *He by Himself has sworn; I on His oath depend,*
> *I shall, on eagle wings upborne, to Heav'n ascend.*
> *I shall behold His face; I shall His power adore,*
> *And sing the wonders of His grace forevermore.*
>
> —Thomas Olivers,
> *The God of Abraham Praise*

3

FOREIGNERS & SOJOURNERS: PITCHING TENTS IN THE PROMISED LAND

Abram took his wife Sarai, his nephew Lot, all of their possessions, and those who became members of their household in Haran; and they set out for the land of Canaan. . . . They arrived in Canaan.

—Genesis 12:5

HOW MANY TIMES, LORD, have I thought *if only I could get there, then all would be well?* How many times have I set my hopes on something and believed that all my problems would be solved if only I could achieve that one thing? How many times have I prayed for the thing I knew would save me, but it fell short?

Sometimes arriving isn't all it's cracked up to be.

Even the promised land isn't the answer to all our hopes, our fears, our dreams, our needs. We don't arrive and suddenly all our problems disappear and the whole world is blessed and made right. It doesn't work that way. I forget that sometimes. But Sarai reminds me.

She reminds me to be careful where I place my hope, where I believe I'll find my answers.

She reminds me that in all my frantic prayers and strivings, in all my grasping for that one thing, the promised land is still a poor substitute for the God of promise. Because it is not the land that was promised that is filled with wonder. Wonder is found in the God who promised.

I imagine it happened something like this.

Sarai Tells Her Story

A land of our own. A land God himself would show us. A promise fulfilled, a new start, a new dream, a new life.

Ah, I had such hopes that our arrival in Canaan would make everything right. We would settle here, make a home, have the children God promised us. It was supposed to make sense once we arrived.

But it hasn't happened that way.

There is no child. There is no home, no settling at all. And the land is full of Canaanites. In the promised land, I am but a foreigner, a sojourner.

After traveling hundreds of miles from Haran, we came to Canaan. *"Elohim* has shown me this is the place," my husband said.

And I thought that meant we were done traveling. I thought there would be no more walking, packing, no more dusty days, no more tent-filled nights.

I was wrong.

I stand here now in the land God promised us. My sandals are cracked, worn. My back hurts. My soul does, too. I look over the land, the rolling hills, the long plains, the settlements crouching like old men around a fire.

"There!" Abram points.

A great oak rises from the earth. The tree of Moreh at Shechem.

"Wait here," Abram tells us. So we wait. He is gone far into the evening.

I cook dinner in our travel pans. I serve stew in our travel pots. I wait in our tent-for-travel and sew travel clothes by the fading light.

I sit alone, so no one hears my sigh.

Just as twilight surrenders to encroaching night, he returns. His face almost glows, and I wonder if I can finish a few more stitches by the light of his eyes.

He smiles at me.

I nearly smile back.

He comes and sits by my side.

I smell the woodsy aroma of burned oak. I see the slight dusting of ash on his brow. I know this look. I know this scent. I lift my hand, barely touch the spattering of gray remnants of fire. Words fumble in my mouth like pebbles tossed in a stream. "Did he . . . did he come to you? Did he speak?"

My Abram reaches toward me, his hand cups the back of my neck. Then he draws my face toward him until our foreheads meet, rest together, and mine too bears the soot. His voice is but a whisper. "Yes. The Lord appeared to me."

My breath stops.

"And he told me that he will give this land to our offspring." He moves back, away from me, and his gaze travels out the tent door. "Someday, this will all be theirs."

I let out my breath. Theirs. *Not ours? Why not ours?*

I have no offspring.

I swallow the stone lodged in my throat. "We . . . we will make our home here then?" *At least tell me I have come home.* I want to settle down, make this place all God has promised. I want to be home at last. Then all will be well, as it should be.

Isn't that what God promised to us? To me?

Abram's next words crush me, squeeze like insidious poison into my soul. "No, my love." He looks at me as if he has no idea that I have been waiting for the moment when I could unpack my pots, arrange my furnishings, settle into the promise of *Elohim*. He stands and moves toward the tent opening, his eyes again glance outward, toward the land. It is lit now only by starlight.

"I have built an altar under the great oak." His voice is firm, unwavering, as he turns back toward me. "But that is all we will build here. Tomorrow we will move on toward the hills east of Bethel. There we will pitch our tents."

Always the tents. How can we have arrived and yet still live only in tents?

"From there we will continue toward the Negev."

I press my lips together so nothing will escape. I am afraid of what I might say. *This* was supposed to be the promised land. *This* was supposed to be where all was made right again. *This* was supposed to be the end of travels and tents and trials.

How could it be only the beginning?

How could this life of the sojourner be all that the promise means?

Elohim promised land.

He promised descendants.

Was the promise less? Or could it be that the promise is more than land, more than a child?

Could it be that this promise is even more than I ever dreamed?

Waiting for Wonder

Sometimes, getting where you want to go is not the answer you hoped it would be. Markus Persson, the founder of Minecraft, discovered this truth. A year after he sold his company to Microsoft for $2.5 billion, he Tweeted, "The problem with getting everything is you run out of reasons to keep trying, and human interaction becomes impossible due to imbalance." Two minutes later, at nearly three in the morning, he followed that Tweet with another: "Hanging out in Ibiza with a bunch of friends and partying with famous people, able to do whatever I want, and I've never felt more isolated."[1]

I ponder these thoughts as I imagine Sarai's arrival in the promised land. I consider what it means to finally arrive in the place God has promised and find it is not everything one dreamed or hoped. "When Jesus calls us, he does not guarantee the future or even tell us what it will be like," says scholar R. Kent Hughes when commenting on Genesis 12.[2]

Even when we get there, we can't kick back, settle in, and assume the hard journey is over. I should know this. After eleven years of trying to having a baby, I finally held my newborn girl in my arms. She was beautiful, with pink cheeks, a head full of soon-to-be-curly hair, perfect little fingers, toes . . . vocal cords. She yelled at the top of her lungs for three nights straight after she was born. Nothing appeased her. She had opinions, and she let them be known. I didn't sleep for seventy-two hours.

Having a new baby was not the cream-colored, angels-singing, everything-is-a-picture-perfect painting that I had envisioned. Now, as a teen, my daughter is still beautiful, fierce, determined, and a reminder of what it really looks like to live in the promises of God.

Sometimes it means you have no rest, no pillow on which to lay your head.

To come to the place God has called us does not mean we've arrived at peace, perfection, sweetness, and light. It means we are sojourners, we are foreigners. We arrive, but we are still living in tents.

And that's the way it is meant to be.

Sojourners and Foreigners

Sarai's arrival in Canaan did not result in settling down or making a home, as she'd done in previous lands. She had been settled in Ur, and the Bible specifically points out that the family "settled" in Haran (Genesis 11:31). But when they arrive at the destination God had for them, they didn't settle at all. Instead, Abram traveled from site to site throughout the land. First he made his way to Shechem, then after God promised the land to Abram's descendants, Abram continued south toward the hills east of Bethel. There Abram again did not settle but rather "pitched his tent" (Genesis 12:8). Next, he traveled south to the arid plain of the Negev, its landscape a stark contrast to the fertile, well-watered lands of Haran and Ur. As if to underscore the transitory nature of their arrival in Canaan, Genesis 12:9 includes "making and breaking camp as he went." Then a famine struck and "Abram went down toward Egypt to live as an immigrant" (Genesis 12:10).

As if the constant movement wasn't enough, the Bible also tells us, "The Canaanites lived in the land at that time" (Genesis 12:6). The Canaanites consisted of various fierce and powerful nations whose religions included promiscuity, prostitution, and in some instances, child sacrifice. Abram and Sarai were peaceful shepherds, longing for a child, who followed a radically different God than did the Canaanites. In every way, they were foreigners in a foreign land.

Recently, I had lunch with Terri, a friend who grew up in a military family. Her younger years were filled with moves to various military bases. Later, when she married, her husband's job caused them to move around the country several times. Each time she had to close her business as a real estate agent and start again in the new location. "The other day I counted how many times I've moved," she told me. "Seventeen."

That's a big number. I thought of Sarai living in tents.

Then my friend smiled at me. "I've learned to never say never," she quipped. "Oregon taught me that."

"Oregon?"

"Never thought God would send this Georgia-and-Texas girl to live in Oregon," she said with her Southern-tinged accent. "But he did. God's taken me to places I never thought I'd be, including here in California." Then she began talking about the day Jesus would come back and the Bible's promises of the future would come true. She spoke with passion and hope and a confidence in the work of God that helped me see beyond the here and now and into the wonder of what will be.

She helped me see Sarai's journey.

Hebrews 11:8-10 tells us,

> By faith Abraham obeyed when he was called to go out to a place that he was going to receive as an inheritance. He went out without knowing where he was going. By faith he lived in the land he had been promised as a stranger. He lived in tents along with Isaac and Jacob, who were coheirs of the same promise. He was looking forward to a city that has foundations, whose architect and builder is God.

41

Just like Sarai, just like Terri, we are not meant to settle for a place. We are sojourners, not just in Canaan, but in this life. We don't build spiritual houses in this life because even as we live in the shadow of promises in the here and now, the true fulfillment is yet to come. Receiving eternal life, having a place prepared just for us, seeing the architect and builder face to face, receiving complete healing, realizing full joy, becoming all we were created to be, participating in the beautiful banquet of the Lamb: they are all promised to those who believe. In this life, we face death, we struggle with health, we weep, we go hungry, we sin. We live in the promised land of the grace of God, of all that he's done for us, of a restored relationship with him, but we live in tents. We live in the "not yet" of the ultimate promises.

We live like Sarai, as sojourners.

"The security we crave would teach us to rest our hearts in this world. . . . Our Father refreshes us on the journey with some pleasant inns, but will not encourage us to mistake them for home," says C. S. Lewis in *The Problem of Pain*.[3]

And while we live in the promise of God's grace now, this is not home. We are foreigners. We forget that sometimes. But this is Canaan, where angry and powerful people fiercely oppose biblical truth. This is Canaan, where promiscuity, prostitution, and child sacrifice abound. Peaceful shepherds who follow a radically different God are strangers in a strange land.

We live like Sarai, as foreigners.

Arriving in a life of God's grace and forgiveness is not the end of all our troubles. We cannot settle here, build comfortable homes, and expect everything to be as we want it to be. So how do we live in faith as sojourners and foreigners in this life? R. Kent Hughes says, "The authentic life of faith demands that we be pilgrims in this world.... Everything around us tells us to hunker down, save everything, hedge ourselves about with every protection. Our natural desires are for more comforts. Our culture celebrates great homes and dynastic families. But God's Word says otherwise, instructing us to 'seek the things that are above,' where Christ is ..." (Colossians 3:1-4).[4]

Where Christ is. I turn the phrase over in my mind. I taste it, savor it. I know that Sarai's arrival in Canaan was not the answer to all her troubles. It was but a step on the journey of God's will. It was not the end or the answer. So I see I must return again to the promise to Abram. I must see it with new eyes, a new heart. I must look at Sarai's journey and again discover my own.

What did the promise really mean? To him and to Sarai? What do God's promises really mean to me?

What Is the Promise?

In Genesis 12:1-3, God says, "Leave your land, your family, and your father's household for the land that I will show you. I will make of you a great nation and will bless you. I will make your name respected, and you will be a blessing. I will bless those who bless you, those who curse you I will curse; all the families of the earth will be blessed because of you."

I notice something startling as I read it again. God gives Abram an instruction, and then he gives a flurry of promises:

I will show you. . . .
I will make of you . . . and will bless you.
I will make your name. . . .
I will bless. . . .

A shiver runs up my spine as I read "I, I, I, I." The promise is not a place. The promise is a person! It is a relationship with God himself. In these promises, God is saying, "I will be your God." He is promising his presence.

And suddenly I see it was never about the place at all. It wasn't about getting somewhere. Instead, it was about calling Abram and Sarai into a unique and special relationship with the God of the universe. And that relationship would result in the blessing of all the families of the earth.

It is no different for us. When we believe the promise is a place, when we think that our problems will be solved by arriving "there," when we chafe at being sojourners and foreigners in this life, we miss the true promise: a unique, intimate, walking-through-Canaan with the person of Jesus Christ.

He is the promise. We do not travel alone. When we stand at the great oak of Moreh and the Canaanites are fierce, he is our God. When we pitch our tents in the dry hills of discouragement and rejection, he is our God. When we travel into the arid deserts of fear and disappointment where no good thing seems to grow, he is with us.

That is the promise.

He is the promise.

And because of that, we can be a blessing to the whole world.

Who Is This God?

I ponder this God who is the promise and I ask again, what does it look like to live in faith as a foreigner and sojourner through this life? What does it mean to live in tents?

Jesus said, "Foxes have dens, and the birds in the sky have nests, but the Human One has no place to lay his head" (Matthew 8:20).

We want so much for God to give us security. Health, wealth, stuff, and riches. And instead he whispers, "Follow me" where we may have none of that.

And I am confronted again with the saddest story in the New Testament. A young man desired to do what was right. He followed God's rules, he loved his neighbors. And one day, God himself spoke to him face to face. Jesus said, "Sell what you own. . . . Follow me!" (Matthew 19:21; Mark 10:21). It was the same call he gave to Peter and Andrew, to John and James, who left their nets, their security, to follow Jesus. It was the call to be a disciple, to be a close friend to Jesus while he walked the earth at the most unique time in history.

The young man came asking only how to inherit eternal life. And in a single moment, Jesus offered so much more. The man would have touched God in flesh, traveled with the Messiah himself, blessed the whole world through his relationship with the Savior. He might have written books of the Bible. He might have been the main character of stories included in the gospel accounts. We might have known his name.

Instead, he went away sad because he had great wealth. He exchanged the person for the place. And he missed the promise.

I want to weep. He was so close to the most amazing promise of all time.

Like Abram and Sarai, he was called to greatness. "Leave all you have," God told them all. "And I will be your God."

But the young man walked away.

He would not be a sojourner, a foreigner to this life, with Jesus. And so he missed this greatest call of all. He missed the intimacy of a friendship with the living God, with the One who said, "I don't call you servants any longer, because servants don't know what their master is doing. Instead, I call you friends, because everything I heard from my Father I have made known to you" (John 15:15). The rich young man missed his life's mission. He missed knowing God. He missed being a blessing.

And I know that I don't want to miss the wonder of God's will because I'm clinging to the safety of arriving. I would rather live in the tents of promise than the palaces of security. I don't want to walk away sad because I'm afraid to lose health or home or relationships or whatever it is that feels like "there" to me. What in my life might cause me to turn away from my life's mission, from knowing God as a true disciple, from being a blessing to the world? Will I settle for the answer to eternal life, when Jesus is offering the promise of intimacy with him?

Our God is a God who says, "Come to Canaan." He calls us to follow him and have no place to lay our heads. He calls us to the tents of life.

God is the God of the sojourner, not the God of settled security.

God is the God of the foreigner, not the God of comfortable control.

God is the God who knows that all our "if onlys" are empty wishes. And he reminds us that the promise is a person. It's not a place. It's not an answered prayer. It's not having our lives look just the way we want them to look. It's not the house we dreamed of, the perfectly suited job, the flawless spouse, the family we imagined when we were young. It is him. Only him. Emmanuel, God-with-Us.

And he is calling us to follow him to the oaks of Shechem, to the hills outside Bethel, to the great arid plains of the Negev. Wherever he leads us. He is calling us to leave security behind and be his disciples. He is calling us to bless the whole world.

Will you pitch your tent in the promise of his presence?

> *Dear friends, since you are immigrants and strangers in the world, I urge that you. . . . Live honorably.*
>
> —1 Peter 2:11-12

4

FEAR, DECEIT, AND A PROMISE RESTORED: SARAI IN EGYPT

Just before he arrived in Egypt, he said to his wife Sarai, "I know you are a good-looking woman. . . . So tell them you are my sister." . . . Then the LORD struck Pharaoh and his household with severe plagues because of Abram's wife Sarai.

—Genesis 12:11, 13, 17

FAMINE AND FEAR, DECISIONS and deceit, plagues and promises bargained away: it's a strange story. It tells of a husband's betrayal, a failure of faith, and a pharaoh's rebuke. It's set in a foreign culture, in a faraway time, in a land very different from our own.

But the God of this story is our God. He is the same yesterday, today, forever. This is a God who remembers. A God who intervenes. A God who knows our names.

This is a story of that God. My God. And yours.

It is a story of Sarai. But Sarai is silent. She doesn't act. She is the voiceless center of a drama between faithlessness and faith, between deceit and redemption.

It is a story of you and me and everyone who has been called his own. It is our story when we have no voice, when circumstances defy the promises of God, when we wonder how we'll ever get out of a hole not of our own digging.

For Sarai, it may have happened something like this.

Sarai Tells Her Story

*F*amine struck. A famine not only of food, but of faith. It drove us from the land, it drove us from the promise, it drove us to Egypt where a pharaoh reigns.

A pharaoh who collects beautiful women the way I collect blue cloth.

I am his now.

I huddle in his harem and wonder what has become of the promises of *Elohim*. The land is gone, the hope of the child, gone. And this is anything but blessing.

A candle flickers. Soft veils rustle. I smell the pungent scents of oils and lotions, of Susinum and Cyprinum, Stakte and Rhondinium. Myrrh and rose and lily and cinnamon. To me, this room smells like a tomb.

Maybe because I feel as though I am buried here.

What will become of me? And how did it come to this? For a moment, I close my eyes and remember the dry and dusty journey from the arid plains of the Negev. I remember when the land began to change from dirt and dryness to the fertile valley approaching the Nile. It looked promising, hopeful. Until my husband—my *husband*—turned to me and said, "I know you are a good-looking woman. When the Egyptians see you, they will say, 'This is his wife,' and they will kill me but let you live."

My heart turned cold. I pressed my lips together and did not speak. I knew what was coming next. I knew and dreaded it.

"Tell them you are my sister so that they will treat me well for your sake, and I will survive because of you."

We entered Egypt with this lie. I carried it like a pack on my back, heavier than the pots, the ointments, the weight of blue cloth. We dropped the feather-light load of the promise and took up instead this burden of self-protecting fear.

We traveled up the Nile toward the royal capital, saw the grandeur of pyramids newly built, and drew the attention of the Egyptians who lived there.

That's when the princes saw me. They praised me to Pharaoh.

And I was taken.

Rumor is that Abram acquired flocks, cattle, donkeys, camels, and servants because of me. Female donkeys even, the most prized of the livestock. And camels, which are the symbol of great riches. Abram is wealthy now. It has gone well for him because of me.

He is rich in possessions.

He is poor in promises.

He has no wife. I belong to Pharaoh now.

A swath of light cuts across the room. Sabaf, the eunuch, enters the chambers. He glances left, then right. I shrink into the shadows. But his gaze falls on me anyway.

His eyes widen. Do I see fear?

He comes toward me, his eyes now averted. He scratches his arm, his neck. "Pharaoh has called for you."

My breath stops. The time has come. Pharaoh, king of all Egypt, he who is called a god, my new master, has summoned me. Who will save me now?

I follow Sabaf from the room, down a long hallway. He continues to scratch his arms, neck, chest. It seems strange, but I do not question him. I dare not say a word.

We continue, but not toward the bedchamber. We walk toward the throne room. I bow my head as we enter, yet I can still see Pharaoh on his throne. He does not glance my way. He has eyes only for the man in front of him. I would not want to be that man.

I draw closer. I look up.

Abram!

He almost peeks at me. I know that look. It is a look of shame.

Pharaoh leans forward. "What's this you've done to me?" His voice booms through the throne room. His scepter points toward me. "Why didn't you tell me she was your wife?"

He knows. He knows and he is angry.

Pharaoh reaches up and scratches his neck. "Why did you say, 'She's my sister,' so that I made her my wife? Now, here's your wife. Take her and go!"

Go?

No punishment? No prison? No death?

Pharaoh is afraid.

He does not look at me as his men hurry me and Abram from the throne room. They do not touch us.

I see the light of day. I see the sun glinting off the Nile. I see merchants and slaves, pyramids and carts. I see Egypt and I am not afraid. I am saved.

I do not belong to Pharaoh after all. I don't belong to Abram either. *Elohim* has redeemed me. He has made me his own.

Because only he remembers who I truly am. He delivered me from the gods of the world, the rulers of this age.

He knows my name.

I am his.

Waiting for Wonder

I ponder this disturbing event in Sarai's life. I imagine her waiting in the shadows of Pharaoh's harem, wondering what will become of her. I study the passage. I read the commentaries. My brow furrows as scholar after scholar talk about Abram, his faith (or lack of it), his destiny, his actions, his schemes.

No one speaks of Sarai. And Sarai doesn't speak for herself.

In the *NIV Application Commentary*, John Walton says, "As Abram sits alone and vulnerable in his tent in Egypt, the promises are in shambles, the covenant dangles from a frayed thread: no land, no family, nothing that looks even remotely like blessing."[1] Bruce Waltke says, "Pharaoh's officials . . . praised her to Pharaoh. This is probably more than Abraham has bargained for."[2] Scholar Iain M. Duguid concurs: "Far from safeguarding the promise, Abram's crafty strategy nearly destroyed the whole plan. . . . [But] circumstances, folly, and even sin would not stand in the way of God's purpose to make Abram a great blessing."[3]

Everyone focused on Abram. Everyone, that is, except God.

He Knows Your Name

Genesis 12:15 says, "The woman was taken into Pharaoh's household." The woman—a generic term. She was a faceless, nameless entity with no identity; an object, a possession. Abram had called her "sister," Pharaoh and his household call her "woman."

And then God intervened. Verse 17 says, "Then the LORD struck Pharaoh and his household with severe plagues because of Abram's wife Sarai." Here, Sarai was called by both her name and her proper identity. She was Sarai; she was not woman. She was Abram's wife; she was not sister.

To Abram, she was a pawn in a game to keep him safe. To Pharaoh, she was a pretty, new acquisition. To God, she was Sarai, Abram's wife, precious in her own right.

Even though Sarai was an essential partner in God's plan to redeem and bless the whole world, the text doesn't say that God rescued her to accomplish his promise. As Kenneth Mathews asserts, "Reportedly, the passage insists that the events turn on account of Sarai (vv. 13, 16, 17)."[4]

We want to make it about Abram. God makes it about Sarai.

And she didn't have to say a word.

God to the Rescue

Nor did she have to take action to save herself. She couldn't, not in that culture. At that time women were considered possessions, and it was not uncommon for powerful men to dispose of a beautiful woman's husband in order to claim her for himself. Abram was well aware of this practice, so his fear for his life was well-founded. He knew he could not protect Sarai. So he came up with a plan. If others thought she was his sister, as her brother he could bargain for her bride-price. Perhaps he thought he could keep the bargaining going long enough to escape.

Whatever he thought, his plan resulted in Sarai's being taken into Pharaoh's harem. Pharaoh was known for acquiring beautiful women. This was so much his practice that the princes were accustomed to scouting out these women and reporting them to the king, as we see in our story. Abram received riches; Sarai was sold.

She was in an impossible situation where she had no power to rescue herself. She was owned by Pharaoh, the most powerful man in the land. Egyptian culture even believed him to be a god.

Then, in a foreshadowing of what would happen to Sarai's descendants in the centuries to come, God sent plagues to rescue his chosen from the grip of Pharaoh. For Sarai, the plagues came against Pharaoh and his household, and he let Sarai go. For the Israelite nation hundreds of years later, God would send ten plagues against Pharaoh, his household, and all Egypt to rescue his chosen people. God's people, in both Sarai's case and in the exodus, were delivered from another "god" by a God who is more powerful, more determined, more faithful than anything that could stand in his way. He did not abandon Sarai or his people to Egypt. He rescued his own.

Everything Abram did put Sarai, and seemed to put God's promise, in peril. Abram left the promised land and entered a land where a pharaoh was a god. Then through deceit, he lost his wife, the mother of the promise. Through faithlessness, he betrayed his partner.

She had no husband, she had no land, she had no hope for the promised son of Abram. And God saw her, called her by name, rescued her, restored her.

This is a God who is not thwarted by the betrayals, mistakes, fears, or hurtful actions of others. Others may create difficult circumstances in our lives. We may even create the difficult circumstances ourselves. But none of that can derail God's promises. God can make things right.

And he does so because we are his, and he has claimed us for his own.

I Am Felicia

Not long ago I held a tiny bunny against my shoulder. Her soft fur tickled my skin, her nose twitched. She wiggled and climbed higher until her cheek pressed into mine, her face so close that she could smell my breath. She breathed in, relaxed. Her heart beat with mine.

I knew it was a divine moment.

I whispered in her ear and remembered where she came from. She was found cold and shivering in a tiny burrow in someone's backyard. A little baby bunny with a few long, lion-hairs sticking from between her big ears and mud obscuring her white-and-brown fur. She huddled abandoned and alone, much too young to be without her mother.

She could not save herself.

But then a hand reached into her burrow, a hand bigger than she was. She trembled, cowered to the far side of the dirt and rock. She almost bit the hand, almost drew blood. But fingers closed gently around her, and the hand brought her out of hiding and into the light.

The hand rescued her.

And now, after a trip to the rabbit rescue center, to an adoption event at the pet store, and to my home, she's not alone anymore. She's mine. She no longer cowers in the back of burrows. She doesn't need to be afraid. Instead, she's growing, exploring, and breathing deeply from the breath of the one who loves her.

And she has a name. Felicia.

As I hold her close, I am reminded of what God has done for me. I, too, have been rescued, and now I long to be so close that I can smell the breath of God, feel his heartbeat, and soak in his love for me.

I was alone. I was afraid. I would have died there in my burrow, in my sin. But then hands reached out; nailed hands reached out on a wooden cross. They found me, brought me into the light. I was rescued, cared for, adopted into the family of God. I was made his own.

As I hold Felicia in my arms, her face close to mine, I think about Jesus, his arms stretched wide. I think of his blood shed for me. I think of my sin covering me like mud from a hovel and how that scarred hand came into my dark burrow and rescued me.

I am Felicia, rescued, adopted, and held close to the beating heart, the warm breath, of the God who loves me enough to make me his own, no matter the cost.

No matter who others say you are, God knows who you really are. He does not play games. He is bent on your rescue.

No matter how badly faith fails, God does not forget his promises or fail to bring about his will.

No matter how helpless you are or how you've been betrayed, God can bring blessing and restoration to your life.

There is no hole too deep, no inner room too distant for him to find you.

A flawed friend, spouse, parent, sibling, boss, coworker doesn't define you. No pharaoh owns your life.

You are God's. He has rescued you from the dark hole of fear, from the shadowy recesses of a false god's palace. He has made you his own.

Crawl nearer. Turn your face to his. Breathe deeply of the breath of the God who loves you. He holds you in his hand.

Who Is This God?

Who is this God who rescues us from the harem of Pharaoh, who stops at nothing to reach into our shadows and bring us into his light? Who is he who calls us by our name and tolerates no deception?

He is the God of Sarai.

He is the God of rescued rabbits.

He is the God who stopped a crowd to look a healed woman in the face, to call her by her true name. Matthew 9, Mark 5, and Luke 8 tell about a woman who had been bleeding for twelve years. No doctor could heal her. She had no money, no cure, no hope. Like Sarai, she was caught in the dark shadows of circumstances that shut her away from her most precious relationships. She was untouchable. She could not go into the temple. And this disease was as powerful in her life as Pharaoh himself.

But she saw Jesus. She wiggled her way through the crowd that day. She touched the hem of his robe. And she was healed. She was free.

At that moment, she had everything she had come for, everything she hoped for.

She was finished.

Jesus was not.

He stopped the crowd. He turned. He looked around carefully to find her. And he said to her, "Daughter, your faith has healed you; go in peace, healed from your disease" (Mark 5:34).

He called her Daughter. He called her his own.

Daughter, loved one, precious one, dear one. Daughter, the one you would give anything to save.

That's who she was.

That's who we are.

Healing is not enough. Rescue is not complete without restoration. Sarai was sent away with Abram only when her right relationships with him and with God were restored. The woman called "Daughter" was sent away only when Jesus had stopped the crowd to restore her to the community and to himself. Only when she was called by her true name—Daughter.

When no one saw her for who she was, Jesus did. Even now we refer to her as "the woman with the issue of blood." But Jesus didn't call her that. He called her Daughter. And he made her whole.

So when you are waiting in the dark, when hope seems lost, when circumstances are beyond your control, when God's promises seem like a distant dream, he is coming to rescue you. You are his precious one.

All you may be wanting is your situation fixed, but he is offering so much more. He will stop the world to look you in the face, love you, and call you his child.

No matter where you are, what you've done, what's been done to you, he names you as his own. You will be called out of Pharaoh's harem and set free.

Reach out to touch the hem of his cloak, and wait for your redeemer.

> *Turn your eyes upon Jesus,*
> *Look full in His wonderful face,*
> *And the things of earth will grow strangely dim,*
> *In the light of His glory and grace.*

> —Helen H. Lemmel

5

The God Who Takes Too Long: Sarai's Desperate Plan

Sarai, Abram's wife, had not been able to have children. Since she had an Egyptian servant named Hagar, Sarai said to Abram, "The LORD has kept me from giving birth, so go to my servant. Maybe she will provide me with children." Abram did just as Sarai said.

—Genesis 16:1-2

I KNOW THE COLD, EMPTY chill of desperation. The heavy weight in your gut that steals faith, quenches dreams. Vision darkens. Hope dies.

You're afraid and God has taken too long.

You've prayed.

You've believed.

You've trusted.

God has not moved. Nothing changes. The insidious weight of the wait becomes too much to bear.

Fear hisses. Doubt slithers. Faith falters.

And in the silence of the heavens, you listen to baser whispers that creep through your mind: "Did God really say. . . ?"

Did God really promise?

Is God really there?

Does God really love me?

"Hope delayed makes the heart sick," says Proverbs 13:12. And sometimes, in the sickness of the heart, you do something immensely foolish.

I've been there, in that questioning, hope-delayed-until-my-heart-is-crying place. Sarai had, too. I do not condemn her. I cannot wag my finger, cluck my tongue, shake my head at her. Desperation can make you crazy. It can make you a fool.

I am like Sarai. And so I tremble at the choice she made from desperation, from anger, from heartbreak, from fear.

Perhaps it happened something like this.

Sarai Tells Her Story

*T*oo long. It has taken too long. And now it's too late for me. We have been ten long years in the land of Canaan, the land of the promise. Ten barren years.

And there is no child.

I knead the bread for the day. My fingers sink deep in the dough. It is warm and sticky and full of life.

I am full of death.

Elohim has renewed his promise to Abram. He has made a binding covenant. A smoking vessel with a fiery flame passed between the split-open animals Abram prepared for the Lord, his God. A covenant made by *Elohim* alone, unbreakable. Secure. Eliezer from Damascus, who runs our household, will not be the heir. A son will come from Abram's own loins.

But not from mine.

I have waited ten years. Now I am dried up, a withered branch that can no longer bear fruit. A dried crust from too-old bread.

Too old.

All the smoke and fire cannot change that. I have lost all hope that the promises of God will come through me. I pull my hands from the dough and stare at the fine lines in my skin, covered now with flour. Old hands, old skin, shaking palms.

But there is still hope for Abram.

I have a plan.

There is a custom among the peoples of the land. A barren wife may give her maidservant to her husband to bear children for her. She must give him a second wife.

I must give him a second wife.

I choke on the plan. Hate it. But there is no other way. I will give my maidservant to Abram. I will give away part of my heart.

I will swallow the bile that rises from this plan of mine. I will clench my teeth and close my eyes. I will do what must be done to get what I must have.

I glance across the field. I see her there, Hagar, my servant from the spoils of Egypt. Part of the price Pharaoh paid to see me gone. She bends over, dips a bucket in the stream.

She is young, and slim. Dark and lovely.

She has good hips for bearing.

She is mine. I can do with her as I please. And maybe, just maybe, something good will come from Egypt after all.

So I wait through one more long day, until the dusk brushes the sky and gives way to night. Then I call Hagar to me.

And I call Abram.

He comes to me across the starlit path. Tent flaps rustle. My heart slams against my chest. Still, I force the words from me, like weapons aimed at him. Aimed at *Elohim*.

"The Lord has kept me from giving birth, so go to my servant. Maybe she will provide me with children." I shove Hagar toward him.

And he takes her. Just like that, he takes her to his tent.

I almost call after them. Almost. But instead I bite my tongue and turn away. I have done what I must. *Elohim* will not give me a son. I must get one for myself.

If God will not act, I will.

I cannot sit here and do nothing.

Ten years is too long. It is time for the promise to be mine. Long past time.

God has failed me.

Perhaps Hagar will not.

I fall to my knees and sob behind a dead, dry bush.

Waiting for Wonder

In Egypt, Abram betrayed Sarai and the promise by choosing his plan over trusting God. Back in Canaan, Sarai betrayed Abram and the promise by choosing her plan over trusting God.

After ten years in Canaan, in the land that God had promised, Sarai still didn't have a son. She was seventy-five years old and most likely past menopause.

Simply put, she lost hope and chose to get what she wanted in the only way she knew how. In the previous chapter in Genesis, God had cemented his covenant to Abram. In Abram's time, two parties would enter into a solemn covenant by splitting the carcasses of sacrificed animals in half and then walking between the two halves. Both parties in the covenant relationship would pass between the halves of the animals to say, in effect, "May I be like these slaughtered animals if I break my promise."

In Abram's case, only God passed between the split animals. Genesis 15:17-18 says, "After the sun had set and darkness had deepened, a smoking vessel with a fiery flame passed between the split-open animals. That day the Lord cut a covenant with Abram." The smoking vessel represented the presence of God. God and Abram did not enter into covenant together, each taking responsibility for part. Instead, God took all the responsibility for the covenant, for the promise of land and descendants as numerous as the stars, upon himself. Abram promised nothing. Nothing was required of him for God to fulfill his promises.

But even as God confirmed the covenant, nothing changed in their circumstances. They were still foreigners in the land. Sarai was still not pregnant. And a confirmation of the promise was not enough to lift the burden of the long wait.

Author Arthur Pink says, "But waiting is just what the natural heart finds it so hard to endure. Rather than wait man prefers to take the management of his affairs into his own hands and use human expediencies to give effect to the Divine promise."[1]

So Sarai took on the responsibility of accomplishing the covenant that God had just claimed as fully his responsibility. God said, "I will do this." Sarai said, "I'm going to make sure."

Her actions were consistent with the culture of her time. On a tablet archaeologists have discovered from ancient Mesopotamia we can read about a marriage situation very like Sarai's. It tells us that if the wife fails to bear children, she must provide a slave girl to her husband to bear children for her. The actual marriage contract (translated) reads, "If Gilimninu bears children, Shennima shall not take another wife. But if Gilimninu fails to bear children, Gilimninu shall get for Shennima a woman from the Lullu country . . . as concubine. In that case, Gilimninu herself shall have authority over the offspring."[2] A woman from the Lullu country would have been a slave girl, much like Hagar.

Sarai's culture said that giving Hagar to Abram was the right choice. God said it was not. Directly following the creation of Eve, Genesis 2:24 says, "This is the reason that a man leaves his father and mother and embraces his wife, and they become one flesh." God had chosen one man and one woman to become one flesh. Up until now, Abram and Sarai, despite the culture around them, had adhered to that standard. Abram was a rich man. He'd acquired many goods and people in Egypt. Culturally, concubines would have been expected. But until now, he had only Sarai for a wife.

But Sarai sacrificed that unique, exclusive relationship with her husband because in the long wait she had lost all hope that the promise would come through her. Like Abram as he entered Egypt, she chose her own schemes over a God she didn't believe would come through.

Blaming God

The first words she spoke to Abram highlight the crux of the problem: "The LORD has kept me from giving birth" (Genesis 16:2). She had no doubt of the power or presence of Abram's God. She did not question his existence or his ability. She questioned his care. "God has done this terrible thing to me," she said. She submitted to the reality of his power, but not to the reality of his love as presented in the covenant.

The covenant is, at its heart, a promise of love and redemption, a promise that everything will be made right because of God's love for Abram and Sarai, and for us. The entirety of the history of God's people is predicated on the idea that he cherishes us. Through the centuries, he never abandoned Israel. He never gave up. He never revoked his covenant. In Isaiah 49:15, God said, "Can a woman forget her nursing child, fail to pity the child of her womb? Even these may forget, but I won't forget you."

God does not forget. He does, however, sometimes let us wait. And in that interval between promise and fulfillment, in the "not yets" of life, we typically do not lose faith in God's omnipotence; rather we lose sight of his love.

When God took too long for Sarai, she turned to herself. She trusted herself. She wanted to fulfill the promise on her own terms, to make it happen *now*. She could not wait.

So she took over God's job, what he had promised to do. When she lost faith in his love, she didn't want to trust God, she wanted to *be* God. She wanted to be the one who made the promises come true.

She was a lot like Eve.

Too Like Eve

The writer(s) of Genesis intended for us to see the correlation between Sarai's actions in Genesis 16:2-3 and Eve's actions in Genesis 3. In the way that Adam followed Eve into sin, Genesis 16:2 tells us that "Abram did just as Sarai said." In Genesis 16:3, Sarai "took her Egyptian servant Hagar" in the same way that Eve "took some of [the tree's] fruit" in 3:6. Sarai "gave [Hagar]" to her husband with the same Hebrew verb that Eve "gave some [of the fruit]" to hers.

God walks with us in the garden, in the promised land, and even in the wilderness. He gives us his presence just as he gave it to Sarai and to Eve. That does not mean, however, that he gives everything we want when we want it.

Satan tempted Eve with the words, "You will be like God" (3:4). Sarai, too, wanted to take over God's job. God was not doing it well enough, fast enough. So they were tempted, as we are, to be our own gods. We'll get it for ourselves, do it for ourselves, rely on ourselves and our own plans.

Centuries later, God would say of Sarah's descendants, "They have forsaken me, the spring of living water. And they have dug wells, broken wells that can't hold water" (Jeremiah 2:13). Some things never change.

Eve, Sarai, the Israelites . . . you and me. We are all tempted to choose our own flawed shortcuts over waiting for God. Sometimes it just seems easier to trust ourselves and our own plans.

Sometimes we feel as though God has let us down. We don't really believe that God has our best interests at heart.

Sometimes we're not even as patient as a just-turned-four-year-old with her daddy.

Balloons on the Ceiling

I've learned something lately about what it means to have faith in both the ability and love of God during the long wait. My daughter Jordyn taught me that on the day after she turned four.

She bolted in the door as we came home from picking up her sisters from school. She ran into the living room and grabbed the giant Mylar balloon we had gotten her for her birthday. Her favorite princess smiled from the shiny surface of the balloon as the two of them danced around the room. The room with a thirty-five-foot ceiling.

The dancing lasted ten seconds before the ribbon came loose and up, up, up floated the smiling princess.

Jordyn looked up. So did I.

Her brow furrowed. So did mine.

"Well, that's going to take months to come down," said one sister.

"You're never going to get that down. Mylar balloons take forever to lose their air," said another.

Jordyn didn't even blink. "Daddy will get it down."

I knelt beside her. "Daddy's tall, but he's not that tall, honey. He can't reach that."

"Daddy will get it down."

Sister number one sighed. "You could try jumping off the stair railing."

I glared at her.

She grimaced. "Just kidding. But there's no way Dad can get that. There'd have to be like five dads standing on each other's heads."

I paused a moment to try to imagine that.

Jordyn raised her chin. "Daddy will get it. Daddy loves me."

But Daddy wouldn't be home for hours.

During the next three hours (an eternity for a four-year-old), Jordyn played with puzzles, she snacked on a strip of dried fruit, and every so often she glanced up at her beloved balloon still pressed against the ceiling, far out of reach. She waited and watched and waited some more.

And she never tried jumping off the railing.

Three hours later, Daddy came through the door.

"Welcome home." I pointed to the ceiling far above us. "We've got a problem."

"Daddy will get it!" Jordyn shrieked with joy.

I raised my eyebrows and whispered to my husband, "Sorry. We told her it's too high."

Bryan grinned. "No problem. I can get that down."

"What?"

"I have a telescoping pole. I can get that down in a matter of minutes. And even if that doesn't work, I'll figure out something else."

He brought in the long, telescoping rod, duct-taped another pole onto that one, put sticky tape on the end, and minutes later, the impossible was not only possible, but completed. Down, down, down came the balloon at the end of that long stick.

He plucked the balloon from the tape, leaned over, and handed one shiny, smiling princess to Jordyn.

She grabbed it with one hand and threw her other arm around his neck. "Daddy got it!" She gave him a big, smacking kiss on the cheek and laughed.

The rest of us laughed too.

Bryan reached for the balloon. "Now, let's make sure the ribbon doesn't come loose again." He took the ribbon and tied it tight, with two double knots.

A moment later, Jordyn was back to singing and dancing around the living room with her great, big princess balloon.

I watched her and smiled.

No matter what anyone said, no matter how impossible it seemed, Jordyn had complete confidence that her daddy could not only get that balloon off the ceiling, but he would. Because he loved her. She didn't doubt, she didn't fuss, she didn't give up. And she didn't try anything crazy to get it down herself. She just trusted.

Our God is one who may not instantly appear to rescue our balloon from the ceiling of life. There may be long waits when it seems as though nothing is happening and everyone is saying change is impossible. There may be long afternoons when dreams lie far out of reach and the dangling string of hope is beyond our grasp.

We may live ten long years in Canaan with no son to show for it. We may hear the words of promise and see no results. And so there is Hagar, a plan of our own making, a desperate scheme to force God's hand. It seems reasonable. Everyone else is doing it.

But our Father is coming home. Rescue is on its way. We need only to wait, to trust, to believe not only that he can get the balloon, but that he will. He will because we are his precious children, and he loves us.

Who Is This God?

There is something about waiting with our God. He is the God of waiting. Waiting is hard, but somehow it's what God asks of us.

Daniel and the exiles in Babylon were promised they would return to the land of Israel. They waited seven decades. A lifetime. In Babylon, Daniel served four foreign kings who believed themselves equal with God. His friends were thrown into the fire; he was thrown into a den of lions. He remained in exile. Daniel learned to wait.

Mary received the promise about her son from the lips of an angel. It took over thirty years for that son even to begin his public ministry. All that time she waited with the promises of an angel still unfulfilled. Waited, while nothing happened. No Roman overthrow, no popularity, no growing force. Even his ministry looked nothing like what she may have expected. Mary learned to wait.

Jesus' followers received the promise of his return. They expected him to come in their lifetimes. But even through persecution, Roman arenas, and the stoning of saints, Jesus did not return. They died waiting for his promise to be fulfilled. We still wait.

We wait decades, centuries, millennia.

Because for our God, time is not a constraint. This is the God about whom the psalmist said, "In your perspective a thousand years are like yesterday past, like a short period during the night watch" (Psalm 90:4) and Peter wrote, "Don't let it escape your notice, dear friends, that with the Lord a single day is like a thousand years and a thousand years are like a single day" (2 Peter 3:8).

He is the God of the wait. He is the God who calls us to wait in faith. He says to us:

- Wait for the LORD; be strong and take heart and wait for the LORD. (Psalm 27:14 NIV)
- We wait in hope for the LORD; he is our help and our shield. (Psalm 33:20 NIV)
- Be still before the LORD and wait patiently for him. (Psalm 37:7 NIV)
- It is good to wait quietly for the salvation of the LORD. (Lamentations 3:26 NIV)

When hope seems gone. When ten years have passed in Canaan and there is no promised son. When the cold, empty chill of desperation becomes a heavy weight in your gut, remember that time is God's servant. He holds it in his hands.

> *The LORD is waiting to be merciful to you,*
>   *and will rise up to show you compassion.*
> *The LORD is a God of justice;*
>   *happy are all who wait for him.*

> —Isaiah 30:18

6

WHEN PLANS GO AWRY:
HAGAR'S REBELLION

He slept with Hagar, and she became pregnant. But when she realized that she was pregnant, she no longer respected her mistress. Sarai said to Abram, "This harassment is your fault. I allowed you to embrace my servant, but when she realized she was pregnant, I lost her respect. Let the LORD decide who is right, you or me."

—Genesis 16:4-5

WHAT DO YOU DO when all your plans come crashing down around you? What do you do when you've tried to build a life and instead it falls apart? Who is God in the rubble of broken hopes, crumbled dreams? Who is he when everything you've hoped would save you becomes the very thing that causes more pain?

Sometimes life doesn't turn out the way you planned. In fact, it rarely turns out that way. So often we stand hurt and frustrated as our carefully constructed plans are crushed into fine sand, running through our fingers.

Where is God then? Whom do we turn to? How do we trust? And what does it mean to leave the broken parts of life in the hands of our God?

Sarai knew that place of brokenness, of frustration and anger, of hurt and hopelessness. Perhaps it happened something like this.

Sarai Tells Her Story

All I wanted was to build my family, build a life. All I wanted is what every other woman has. Was it really too much to ask? Too much to hope for? Too much to dream?

Maybe it was. I sold my soul, or at least I sold my husband, for a chance at the child I wanted so desperately. I sold everything for a dream that will not come true.

I was a fool. I gave him my maid. He took her.

And now she is with child.

I should be happy, fulfilled, triumphant.

I see her there, walking from his tent, her belly round and vibrant. She touches it with just the tips of her fingers.

And her gaze slides to me. Her chin lifts.

She is happy. She is filled. She is the one who has triumphed.

And I have nothing but her scorn.

It's not fair. It's not right.

She sidles over to me, black hair cut in the Egyptian style, a touch of kohl around her eyes. Kohl! Worn by queens and noblewomen. She wears it now, just the smallest bit to taunt me. She saunters toward me, her hips swaying, her belly so, so round.

She stops, looks me straight in the eye as if we are equals. As if I were the slave and she the master. "I have been sent to inquire about a poultice for my back. I am becoming quite sore carrying his heir."

She says more, but I do not hear it. All I hear is the blood pounding in my ears. My hand flits, instinctively, to my flat stomach. So flat, so . . . so dead. "You are young. Carry the child without complaint."

Her gaze flickers over me. "Perhaps you would understand if you were able to conceive. But since you are not. . . ."

My jaw tightens. "There is much work to be done. Clothes to be washed. Dinner to be prepared."

"I simply cannot."

"You will."

"Abram says—"

"Stop!" My breath is coming sharp and short, bursts of fury, hot in my mouth and nose. I swallow and taste the anger. It rises up until my face flushes with it. I narrow my eyes. "We will see about this. I am still his wife, his first wife. You are nothing but a servant."

"The mother of the heir."

My voice fairly shrieks from me. "A slave. *My* slave! You are nobody. Nothing! You . . ." The words sputter out to silence. I am shaking. My flat, empty, childless stomach turns and writhes. I don't recognize this woman I've become, this screaming harpy. This crazed once only-wife.

Elohim, *where are you? How could you let this happen to me? Can't you see what this woman is doing to me?*

Can't Abram see?

I turn on my heel and march toward his tent. She is still squawking behind me. I do not listen. I do not care what else she says.

She does not follow.

I shove back the flap of Abram's tent with a flourish. I storm inside. He has just come in from tending the sheep. His eyes are wide, innocent. He steps back.

I do not wait for him to greet me. "This harassment is your fault!" I throw the words at him like weapons.

Carefully he sets down the cloak in his hand. But he makes no move toward me. I see the question in his eyes, the confusion, the doubt.

And it fires my fury.

"How can you not see? I allowed you to embrace my servant, but when she realized she was pregnant, I lost her respect." My fists dig into my hips. "She treats me like the dirt in her sandals, like something you shake out and turn your back on. I will not tolerate it. I am your wife!"

He shrugs. He does not understand. He will not intervene. I see it in his face, the tilt of his eyebrows. He will not advocate for me, this man who has done me wrong, who has somehow inspired a slave to defy me.

There is no one left. No one but *Elohim* to take my side. Only the God of Abram will defend me now. I straighten my shoulders.

"Let the Lord decide who is right, you or me." The statement rings through the tent like the falling of a hammer. It reverberates into sudden silence.

God, who kept me from having a child, will judge on my behalf now. He has to. He has to see what he's done to me.

My life has crumbled to dust, like the sands of Canaan, dry and bitter in my mouth. And I have no one left but the God who has withheld his blessing.

Only he will hear my cry.

Waiting for Wonder

Sarai's goal was to build a family through Hagar, to build her life into something strong that would last into the future. The original Hebrew in Genesis 16:2 reads, "Perhaps I shall be built from her." She wanted to build herself up by creating a life that looked as much as possible like the life she believed was valuable. For Sarai, such a life required a son, an heir.

So she sacrificed everything she had—her marriage that had been patterned after the "two shall become one flesh" ideal of creation, her exclusive relationship with her husband, and her maidservant—in an attempt to build the kind of life she wanted.

But people who follow the call of God no longer have the power to build their own lives. In accepting God's covenant and call, both Sarai and Abram released the ability to shape their lives in conjunction with their own goals and ideas of what life should look like.

Loss and Anger

This was a lesson Sarai learned the hard way. Sarai's plan was to gain esteem in the eyes of others by having her maid's child counted as her own. Instead she lost esteem as her maidservant disrespected her.

In Sarai's culture, a woman's status was directly tied to birthing babies. Sarai's plan was to build her status, her reputation, her worth, by using Hagar to overcome the stigma of infertility. She was supposed to be more valued, more respected, more revered once Hagar bore a child for Sarai.

But everything she'd hoped to gain was lost when Hagar became pregnant and used her pregnancy to demean her mistress. She gambled everything she had and lost. Then Sarai had nothing left. Nothing but her anger . . . and her God.

In God's Hands at Last

Sarai's first words were of blame: "This is your fault!" We can almost hear her anger, her frustration, her pain as she lashed out with the bitter accusation. Never mind that the plan was her own. Never mind that it was her desperation that drove her to it. In her mind, Abram had not protected her status as first wife. In their patriarchal society, he had not assured her place in the proper family order.

The plan let her down. Her husband let her down.

The only one left was the God who'd prevented her bearing a child in the first place. It was to him that she returned.

"Yahweh shall judge between me and between you," she declared (in the original Hebrew). Only then, in her anger, frustration, and hurt, was she willing to place her fate in the hands of her God. For the first time, Sarai purposefully let go and called on God to do as *he* saw fit. Her plans, despite their success, had failed. They'd failed her entirely. So now she turned to the One she'd usurped just two verses before. She thrust her pain, her indignation, her failure, her frustration into the hands of God and left it there. God would judge. And she would take whatever he gave.

Her attitude was not ideal. She went to God not with humility, but with fury. She trusted judgment to God not so much because of faith in his character but more because she had nowhere left to turn.

She was a lot like you and me. Sometimes life must go completely awry before we release our manipulations and allow God to stand between us and others, before we allow him to be the judge. Our own plans must crumble around us before we let God build us however he chooses. Our sand castle dreams of what our lives should be must wash through our fingers before we step back and trust God to make us homes of rock.

And that is what he does. We may come in anger, in blame, in hurt and desperation, but God still accepts us. At our wit's end, he is ready to rebuild. The question is, when life falls apart, are we willing to accept what comes through his hands?

Faith When All Is Rubble

I thought about that question recently on the anniversary of the September 11 terrorist attacks in New York (and other cities). I pondered crashing airplanes and toppling towers. I remembered the ache of ash and hopes buried in rubble.

It was a day that changed the world.

And it reminded me of other days, days that changed my world, or days that changed the worlds of those close to me.

Planes still crash into the towers of our lives. There are still aches in ash and buried hope. There are still moments when all we can do is cry and blame and weep and scream. We point fingers and say it is all someone else's fault. And still life is a mess, everything has gone wrong, and every plan to build up has instead resulted in rubble.

What do we do with those moments, those days, those periods of life when we can do nothing to make it better, to make the pain go away? How do we look on with faith? How do we follow God in a broken world, with our broken lives?

My six-year-old son, Jayden, taught me something about that. He was recently diagnosed with type 1 diabetes, an unpreventable, incurable, life-threatening autoimmune disease. It invaded our lives, toppled our towers, and made rubble of all our carefully constructed plans.

But in the midst of the debris, Jayden showed me what faith really is. A couple months after Jayden was diagnosed, the doctor prescribed (and the insurance finally approved) a new device to help measure his blood glucose in a more continuous way. He'd have to wear the device all the time, inserting a fresh sensor into his skin at least once a week. He'd have to carry a receiver and, here's the good news, an iPhone so the data could be sent to his dad's and my phones and we'd be able to monitor him from a distance.

He wasn't very happy about diabetes. And he was even less happy about wearing a pod stuck into his skin with a needle. He didn't want to wear "the pokey thing." That is, until we told him he could have his very own iPhone if he agreed to wear the device. That's all it took to convince him.

His ten-year-old sister was not so thrilled. She'd wanted a phone for years. We kept saying no. In her frustration she blurted out, "I wish I had diabetes!"

And then Jayden did an amazing thing. He didn't tell her "No you don't!" or complain about the difficulties of diabetes. He didn't get mad. He didn't yell. He just looked at her with a bland don't-be-dumb look and said, "God gives you diabetes. You don't just give it to yourself."

I stopped in my tracks. I might have said, "God didn't give you diabetes." But I didn't say that. I couldn't. Because Jayden wasn't blaming God for his diabetes. Instead he was submitting himself to the sovereignty of God in his life. Something sure, solemn, and strong in his voice told me he knew God was completely in control of whatever happened to him, even a lifelong disease. He knew that diabetes had come to him not randomly or through his own choice, but filtered through the hands of the God he loves and trusts.

God could have prevented his diabetes. God did not. And Jayden accepted that fact without being angry and without blaming or trying to excuse God in any way. He let God judge. He let God be God despite the toppling towers of type 1 diabetes. He chose to walk in faith, trusting God in whatever came his way.

And I stood stunned because a little boy said, "God gives you diabetes" not in an I'm-mad-at-God way, but in an I-accept-what-God-gives-me sort of way. He was six years old and he was teaching his sister that you take what God gives you in life and you don't whine about it.

I need that kind of faith.

Sarai did too.

It's the kind of faith summed up by something a dear friend said to me the same week. She was fighting breast cancer and had just had her first surgery to remove lumps. She said, "I think I'm going through some cycles of grief. I feel like this can't be happening to me. Yet why not? Why not me? All of us have struggles. It's what's been given to us in a fallen world, a vehicle for glorifying God and becoming more like Christ."

Our toppling towers are what are given us in a fallen world. They are our vehicles for glorifying Christ. Infertility, diabetes, cancer, a maidservant's disrespect: when our strong towers are on fire and hope crumbles into ash, when our castles of sand wash away and all plans come to naught, that is the time to let God be the judge. It is the time to return to him and let God be the God he is meant to be.

Building the Right Kind of Life

Like Sarai, we strive to build lives that will bring glory to ourselves. But God builds our lives to glorify him. Sarai's plan would have left her no real place in the kingdom story. She would have been insignificant to God's plan of redemption for the whole world. God's strategy was harder, more painful, more frustrating, with a lot more waiting (it would be fifteen more years before Isaac would be born). But through it, Sarai would become the mother of God's people, Israel. She would become the mother of faith.

She wanted to be the constructed, cultural mother of Ishmael. God planned for her to be the true mother of Isaac, through whom the promise would come.

In the same way, when our plans fail, God is waiting to implement his own plan. And his plan is for the promise, for redemption, for love, for the hope of the world to come through us. Through *us*. Not through some surrogate. His grace and salvation are meant to flow through us to the world and to generations to come.

But our plans need to go awry first.

Who Is This God?

Who is this God who allows our plans to become like sand running through our fingers? Who is he who stands by while everything we tried to build crumbles around us?

He is the God who builds.

We work so hard. We labor, we scheme, we work, we plan, we scrape and toil. But sometimes, often, life goes awry anyway. The lives we live are not the lives we planned.

But sometimes the lives we planned must die before we can live the lives God plans for us.

Sarai learned that the hard way.

So did Paul.

The New Testament tells us that Paul built for himself the life of a respected Pharisee. His letter to the Philippians describes it: "I was circumcised on the eighth day. I am from the people of Israel and the tribe of Benjamin. I am a Hebrew of the Hebrews. With respect to observing the Law, I'm a Pharisee. With respect to devotion to the faith, I harassed the church. With respect to righteousness under the Law, I'm blameless" (Philippians 3:5-6).

But after a single encounter with Christ on the road to Damascus (see Acts 22), all of that came crumbling down. Paul lost the carefully constructed life he had built for himself. God built him, instead, a life with meaning. A life that changed the world. Paul's God-built life still affects us to this day, thousands of years later. Had Paul's plan worked out, he would have been nothing but a long-forgotten Pharisee. But the life God built for him blessed the entire world. He became a man who spread the gospel throughout the known world of his time. Thousands were saved because of him. He became a man who would write thirteen of the twenty-seven books of the New Testament. We read his work today. Paul's life is still changing lives. He mattered.

In Philippians 3:7-9, he went on: "These things were my assets, but I wrote them off as a loss for the sake of Christ. But even beyond that, I consider everything a loss in comparison with the superior value of knowing Christ Jesus my Lord. I have lost everything for him, but what I lost I think of as sewer trash, so that I might gain Christ and be found in him."

That's the kind of life to which God is calling all of us. He calls us to a life that matters in the kingdom of God. It may not look like it when everything crumbles around us, when our towers tumble, when the diagnosis is grim. But Sarai's diagnosis was grim too. She was infertile and would remain so for another decade and a half. And yet God built her life into one that changed the world in the great workings of the kingdom.

He can build yours, too.

He is the God who builds.

So when plans go awry, when life falls apart, let God judge. Let God choose. Let God build.

Wait for him. He will change your world, and because of that, you will change the world around you.

> Unless it is the LORD who builds the house,
> the builders' work is pointless.
>
> —Psalm 127:1

7

BECOMING YOUR WORST YOU:
MISTREATING A PREGNANT SLAVE

Abram said to Sarai, "Since she's your servant, do whatever you wish to her."
So Sarai treated her harshly, and she ran away from Sarai.

—Genesis 16:6

MY FISTS CLENCHED, MY face scrunched and turned hot. Then noise like the screech of an old radio burst forth from my mouth: "You will eat those beans! You will eat them right now!" I uncurled one tight fist and slammed my palm down on the dining room table. My kids' eyes grew wide. The baby started to wail.

I started to shake. Who was this crazed woman screaming at her children? The Marlo I knew was calm and reasonable. She had no resemblance to the shrieking maniac who'd temporarily invaded my body and my home.

Most moms I know have experienced what it's like to become the yelling mom they promised themselves they'd never be. All of us know what it's like for stress, pain, and fear to push us into becoming our worst selves. It's horrible, sickening. And we feel helpless to restrain the monster, helpless to repair the relationships damaged in the wake of the beast.

Where is God when you become so much less than he's created you to be? Where is he when you fail, when you blow up your life, when you treat others as they should never be treated? Where is God when you become an unholy mess?

Sarai knew what it was like to become who she never wanted to be. The one who would be commended for her faith in Hebrews 11 was not always faithful. In Genesis 16:6, she was an unrighteous woman who mistreated a pregnant servant.

It may have happened something like this.

Sarai Tells Her Story

*Wh*o is this woman I've become? I don't recognize her. I don't like her. I looked for justice from Abram, for judgment from God.

Instead Abram put the burden of this sassy slave girl, who is pregnant with his child, squarely back on me. "Since she's your servant, do whatever you wish to her," he said. And he walked away. He turned his back.

He turned his back on all my pain, all my hurt, all the scorn and injustice I've ever endured. He threw it right back in my lap, and he walked away.

I left his tent with the fury of my heart unabated. And I could bear the weight of it no longer.

Then I saw her there, by the grinding stone. And I hated her.

So I took all that injustice, all that scorn, all my agony, and I laid it on her. It spilled from me in vile, hateful words and in vile, hateful actions. I beat her with accusations. I beat her with sticks. And I burdened her with more work than any woman can bear.

She ran from me. How could she not? Now she runs back to her homeland, back to Egypt. She carries with her only my scorn . . . and the child of my husband, Abram.

The eyes of *Elohim* are on the downtrodden. He is attentive to their cries. He will hear her. But will he ever hear me again?

From days of old, *Elohim* has judged righteousness by how one treats one's slaves and servants. The righteous act with justice. The righteous treat all with dignity. I have not.

So she's gone.

I do not go after her. I let her go. There is nothing I can do to redeem what I have done.

Everything is lost. I've driven all hope from my tent. No Hagar, no child, no veneer of righteousness to wear like a cloak around me. I am stripped naked. I am fallen. I have soiled my very soul.

I never dreamed I would come to this. I never dreamed I would descend to the place of such unrighteousness.

Who will fix this mess I've made? Who will heal this madwoman I've become?

Elohim, oh *Elohim*, what do you see when you look at me?

Waiting for Wonder

In Sarai's time in ancient Mesopotamia, the Code of Hammurabi stated that if a woman gave her personal maidservant to her husband to have a child and the pregnant maidservant tried to displace her mistress, the mistress could not sell her but should give her a slave-mark and demote her to general slave status. She would no longer serve as the woman's personal maidservant but only as one of the owned slaves of the household.[1] Our text does not say that Hagar tried to displace Sarai, but it does say that Hagar disrespected her. We do not know exactly what that behavior entailed, but we do know that Sarai chose not to follow the Code of Hammurabi. Rather, when Abram put the fate of Hagar in Sarai's hands, Sarai chose to mistreat Hagar.

Sarai had available to her an accepted practice, but instead she foisted her pain on someone else, on the woman who was exacerbating her deepest hurts and insecurities. This tells us that Sarai was not following a rational plan but acting out of her own brokenness. Hagar's pregnancy and disrespect hit Sarai where she was emotionally the most vulnerable. In response, Sarai lashed out with emotionally charged mistreatment.

Furthermore, she no longer called on God to judge. In the verse prior, Sarai had called for God to judge between Abram and herself, but she would not let God judge between herself and her maidservant. Instead, she took Hagar's punishment into her own hands, literally. And in doing so, she became the worst version of herself.

Doing Wrong

What did Sarai do to Hagar exactly? We don't know. But we do know that the Hebrew for "treated her harshly" in Genesis 16:6 is the same word used by God in Genesis 15:13 (just a few verses prior) to describe how the Israelites would be oppressed as slaves in Egypt. So Sarai's treatment of Hagar was probably not just a onetime slipup or a single harsh word. It most likely included ongoing deprivation, physical abuse, injustice, and harsh, unrelenting work. If so, this behavior certainly indicates that Sarai failed to show any mercy, kindness, or grace to her servant. Her treatment of Hagar was completely devoid of the characteristics of the God she herself turned to for justice in verse 5 when she said to her husband, "let the LORD decide who is right, you or me."

Sarai was the one who was supposed to follow the God of Abram in a culture that worshiped other gods. She was the one who should have been more righteous, not less. But in her insecurity, her anger, her fear, her pain, her hate, she failed. And she became an angry, bitter, hateful, hurtful follower of God.

Her behavior was so bad that Hagar ran away.

Nothing Left but Brokenness

When Hagar ran, Sarai lost everything. She had already given away her exclusive relationship with her husband. Now she had lost not only her maidservant and the baby that servant was carrying but also her righteous reputation. She had planned on the baby being the answer to her infertility, the eliminator of her shame, and the fulfillment of God's promises. But now, through her own actions, she'd lost all of that. Before, her infertility had caused her disrespect. Now, her own unrighteousness had cost her even more respect. She could not even call on God to judge on her behalf.

How like you and me! When someone rubs up against our insecurities or hits us in the place where we are most broken, our natural response is to inflict our pain on the offender.

And we lose everything. We ruin relationships, we wreck our witness of God's grace, we become the worst versions of ourselves.

And there we are, with our hidden guilt, with our broken mess, with our shattered relationships and lives.

What then? Where is hope? Where is God? And what can he do when our lives are in shambles by our own hands?

The Yarn Master

Sarai didn't go after Hagar when the servant girl ran away. Abram didn't go after her either. Both seemed incapable of repairing what they had broken. They sat in their tents, with the shards of their hopes, with the weight of their shame, while a woman pregnant with Abram's child ran for Egypt.

Sarai couldn't bring Hagar back. But God did.

God's messenger found Hagar at a desert spring. Hagar had no intention of returning to Sarai. But God saw her, he cared, and he promised to bring blessing from her pain. All he asked was that she return to, and tolerate, the mistress who mistreated her (Genesis 16:9-11).

Hagar returned, not because Sarai had made promises, but because God did.

God restores what we destroy. God brings people back when we cannot. God gave Sarai, and he gives us, another chance to do right.

We sit in our tents with our ruined lives in our hands, and all the while God is going out to restore what we have broken.

I was reminded of God's power to restore when my daughter Joelle was a toddler.

I stood at the bottom of the steps with a blanket in my hands and tears in my eyes. Light shone through a dozen great, gaping holes in the crocheted blanket that I'd made for Joelle when I was pregnant

97

with her. It was to be a special gift, an heirloom, for her to keep into adulthood. But here it was, filled with holes. And there she was, three steps up with scissors in her hand.

She sniffed and rubbed her nose. "I didn't know."

I closed my eyes. She was right. She didn't know. She didn't understand how special that blanket was, that I couldn't replace it, and that it was meant to be a special gift to her. There were a lot of things that she didn't know.

But there were some things she did know. One was that she wasn't allowed to get the scissors out of the drawer. The other was that she wasn't to play with her blanket. She knew how to do the right thing. She chose to do wrong.

And now her special blanket was filled with holes of her own making.

I took the scissors out of her hand and placed them high up on a shelf. Then I rolled the blanket into a ball.

Joelle chewed her lower lip. "I don't know how to fix it, Mommy."

I sighed. "It looks pretty bad. I'll see what I can do."

She made a big, gulping sob and then ran to her bed and threw herself into the pillow.

I went into the dining room, spread the blanket on a table, and tried to figure out how I might salvage the mess. As I did, I thought about how easy it is to do what we shouldn't and so cut up the special things in our lives.

Sometimes, I'm as foolish as a toddler.

Sarai was too.

And as I stood at the table and planned how to tie yarn together to restore the blanket, I was filled with hope for my own broken blankets of life.

God is the yarn master. He can repair the holes I've made. And he can do it far better than I can patch a crocheted blanket. He can bring new beauty out of what I've destroyed. It won't be the same blanket, but it will be one that is touched by his hands and remade into what he wants it to be.

He can bring blessing out of my belligerence.

He can repair what I have cut in my unrighteousness.

He brings Hagar back. He gives us a second chance to do right.

The Hope Restorer

I've seen ruined blankets restored not only in my life and in Sarai's, but most recently in the life of a friend's son. He was a good kid, kind, likable, fun-loving, with a future full of promise. He was brought up to believe in God, but that belief didn't work its way into the center of his life. So when the pressures of life led to the pressures of gangs, he chose gangs over God.

He wanted friends who made him feel important. He wanted the security of belonging. He wanted the glamour of the gang. So the nice, fun-loving kid with the carefree smile found himself in a car with guns in a drive-by shooting that killed an innocent little kid. Somehow this once-Christian boy became the very worst version of himself. He lost everything: his home, his family, his relationships, his freedom.

Behind prison bars, he could do nothing to make things right. He couldn't restore what he'd broken. He couldn't make it all go away. But God was at work. In jail, God found this young man and restored him. My friend's son repented, and God changed his heart. He's still in prison and will be for decades to come, but prison isn't a place of darkness and despair for him. It's a place where he can share the hope of God with others who have failed and are looking for redemption. It's a place where he can reach out and apologize for the pain he's caused not only the victim's family but also his own.

God is restoring the relationships this young man shattered, and God is bringing a lost boy back to himself. Here is a young man who is becoming whole again, and who is helping other inmates to find hope and healing, not through his own power but through the grace of God.

Because that's what God does. That's who God is. He keeps his promises. Even when we do not. He restores our lives, our families, our hope—even when we've cut up our special blankets, blown up our families with our failures, and are sitting in our tents in shame.

Repent, trust, and be brave enough to hope again. God has not turned away. Even now he is at work.

Who Is This God?

Who is this God who takes our tattered ruins and makes our blankets whole again? He is the God who restores.

This is the God who saved a family of seventy through the man who was sold into slavery by his brothers. Joseph's jealous brothers betrayed him. They became their worst selves. But despite their false accusations, his own imprisonment, and his separation from everyone he knew, Joseph received God's blessing. And years later when a famine swept through Canaan, God saved those very brothers and their families through Joseph. God restored the relationship they had shattered and saved their lives. Through Joseph, God brought a blessing to the whole family of Israel. (See Genesis 37–47.)

This is the God who raised up a mighty king of peace to bless Israel through the son of a woman David stole, whose husband he had killed. David, king of all Israel, took Bathsheba to be his own even though she was married to one of the mighty men in his army. Then he told the commander of his armies to put her husband on the front lines and withdraw from him so that he would be killed. He was killed and David became his worst self, an adulterer and a murderer. Yet God still redeemed the relationship with Bathsheba that David had destroyed. Later she bore a son, Solomon, who would rule Israel in peace and wisdom. Despite David's grievous sin, God brought blessing for others from the ruins of what he'd done. Through David and Bathsheba, God brought a blessing to the whole nation of Israel. (See 2 Samuel 11–12; 1 Kings 2–4.)

This is the God who saved over three thousand people in one day through a man who had denied him three times just days before. When Jesus was arrested, his friend Peter denied three times that he knew him even though Peter had earlier promised that he would die for Jesus. Peter was afraid, and he failed. After the resurrection, Jesus restored Peter. Over a meal of cooked fish, Jesus asked Peter three times, "Do you love me?" and Peter replied, "Yes, Lord!" Soon thereafter, Peter boldly preached and over three thousand came to believe in Christ that day. Jesus restored, and the whole church from that time on has been blessed. (See John 18; 21; Acts 2.)

Joseph's brothers, King David, and the apostle Peter made messes of their lives. They betrayed relationships, they acted in unrighteousness, they failed in their faith. But they also repented. And God restored. He brought hope and blessing to others in the aftermath of great failure.

God brought Hagar back. He brings people back together. He repairs what we've broken and makes us whole again. This would be the last time Sarai proposed her own plan, the last time she took matters into her own hands, the last time she tried to play God.

She was to become a new person after this, with a new name and a renewed promise. God would take the shambles of her life and create beauty and blessing.

So, for those who have failed, who have become their worst selves, who have hurt others and blown up relationships, Isaiah encourages us with these words:

> Listen to me, you who look for righteousness,
>   you who seek the LORD:
> Look to the rock from which you were cut
>   and to the quarry where you were dug.
> Look to Abraham your ancestor,
>   and to Sarah, who gave you birth.
> They were alone when I called them, but I
>   blessed them
>   and made them many.
> The Lord will comfort Zion;
>   he will comfort all her ruins.
> He will make her desert like Eden
>   and her wilderness like the Lord's garden.
> Happiness and joy will be found in her—
>   thanks and the sound of singing. (Isaiah 51:1-3)

Look to Sarai. She failed. She hurt others. She cut all kinds of holes in her own blanket. Yet God restored her and made her whole. He blessed the world through her.

If you are sitting in your tent with the shards of your shattered life, look for righteousness, seek God. He will comfort. He will bring you back to himself. He can still make you who he created you to be.

> *After you have suffered for a little while, the God of all grace, the one who called you into his eternal glory in Christ Jesus, will himself restore, empower, strengthen, and establish you.*

—1 Peter 5:10

8

BECOMING YOUR TRUE YOU: A NEW NAME FOR SARAI

God said to Abraham, "As for your wife Sarai, you will no longer call her Sarai. Her name will now be Sarah. I will bless her and even give you a son from her. I will bless her so that she will become nations, and kings of peoples will come from her."

—Genesis 17:15-16

GENESIS 16 ENDED WITH HAGAR bearing a son for Abram. Not for Sarai, for Abram. The text is clear. It ends with the consequences of Sarai's least-finest hour, on the heels of her lost righteousness and her lost hope. Sarai was excluded and barren and had no cards left to play.

And then chapter 17 opens. But it doesn't open with a reminder of Sarai's failure. It doesn't open with scorn or shame. Instead, the very next scene after Sarai's greatest error begins with God revealing a name for himself that is filled with amazing hope, amazing promise. Not only that, God gives Sarai a new name too. He gives her a new hope, a new promise. Not because she's earned it—hardly!—but because of grace. God follows up Sarai's disgrace not with blame but with blessing. For the first time, she is included in the promises and covenant given to Abram.

God calls Sarai to a new relationship with her God, a full commitment, whole-self, everyday walk with the one who is able to do all that he has promised.

Sarai will be made new.

And that gives me hope. When I think all is lost, when I believe I've failed too badly, when I've become who I never wanted to be, God not only restores, he makes new. He makes me new. God calls me from my worst self to my true self, the self who is fully devoted to him, walking before him every day of my life, becoming the person he created me to be.

For Sarai, it may have happened something like this.

Sarai Tells Her Story

After all these years, Abram's God has spoken of me. His promises include me. And he has named me anew.

It has been thirteen years since Hagar's return, since the birth of Ishmael. Thirteen years of believing that boy was the answer to a promise. Thirteen years of not being able to believe it. Of wondering and being afraid to wonder. Of hoping for something more and telling myself I am a fool for hoping at all.

But I have learned something in these waiting years. I have learned that *Elohim* is enough. I have abandoned my schemes. I have let go of blame. I have simply let go.

I have waited.

And I have never claimed Hagar's child as my own. Ishmael is not my son. Hagar bore him for Abram. Not for me.

And now the boy is on the cusp of manhood.

Perhaps that's why *Elohim* has moved at this time. Abram's God has appeared to him again, with a renewed and fuller covenant. With power and promises. With a call to walk before him and be blameless. Be wholly and fully his.

I long to be his. But I don't know how. All I know to do is accept what he's given.

He has come with a new name for himself and for us. For me. He remembered me.

El Shaddai, the sufficient one, the Almighty, the one who is enough. After all these years, he has become enough for me.

Abram, the father of many. Not just of Ishmael, but of nations.

Sarah. I am Sarah. No longer "my princess," but just "princess." Abram says it is because I will be the mother of kings. Me! A mother. Of kings.

A promise. A test. A new name.

In accepting it, I say I am no longer my own. I say I belong to the master who named me. The master who has denied me a son for all these years. A God who promised and promises again . . . while I am still barren, while I am still shamed, while I can see no way for those promises to be fulfilled. Now, when I am long past the age of childbearing. Long, long past.

Still, I take the name and know that in doing so, I am somehow made new.

Abram, Abraham, laughed at the thought. I just shake my head. And I wonder and am afraid to wonder. I hope and tell myself I am a fool.

But fool or no, I am no longer Sarai.

I am Sarah.

And I belong to El Shaddai.

Waiting for Wonder

Nearly twenty-five years had passed since Abram and Sarai left Haran. Two and a half decades since they chose to obey God's call and move to the promised land. Three hundred months of living with a promise unfulfilled. Three *hundred* months of Sarai *not* being pregnant. And now it was long too late.

It was into this moment that God stepped and renewed a promise that was once unlikely but was now impossible. It was into the long-standing barrenness that he came to make absolutely clear that Ishmael was not the heir of the promise. El Shaddai did not need to work with only what was possible. Rather, he chose the way of the impossible. And here for the first time he specifically included Sarah in the promise. There would be no mistake, no misunderstanding: the promised son would be born of Sarah.

Then, in the face of the impossible promise, God made his call. For the first time the covenant would go beyond God making promises and would extend to the process of true relationship-building with the God of the promise.

God gave them a new name for himself: El Shaddai. This was the first step of their new, binding relationship. Then he called them to walk blamelessly, or wholly, before him. He called them into a whole-life, whole-self relationship with him. He asked them to enter into a binding covenant relationship with El Shaddai, a relationship so new and radical that it required a name change for both.

I pause here for a moment and ponder new, deep, radical, every-single-day walking with the One who is enough. I consider a call to relationship before the promise is fulfilled. A call to intimacy when the promise seems more impossible than ever.

That is when we are called deeper. That is when God says to walk before him with a new devotion. That is when he changes our names.

El Shaddai

It is significant that before God called Abram and Sarai to walk intimately with him, before they became Abraham and Sarah, he first revealed a new name for himself; he gave them a deeper, more intimate glimpse of his character and being. The name *El Shaddai* appears for the first time in the patriarchal narratives here when Abram was ninety-nine years old. The Lord appeared to him and the first words God said were, "I am El Shaddai." We do not know for certain what name Abram and Sarai used for God prior to this. (I have used *Elohim*, the plural of the generic *El* that is used throughout Genesis. The Canaanite pantheon of the time also used *El* to refer to their highest god.)[1]

The etymology and meaning of *Shaddai* are obscure. It is usually translated "God Almighty," but in the Pentateuch (Genesis 28:3; 35:11; 43:14; 48:3-4; Exodus 6:3) there is always a connection with the promise of descendants when using the name, a connotation of God being able to make fertile what is barren and overcome obstacles to fulfill his promises. There's an idea of "God who is able" or "God who is sufficient" even in the face of seeming impossibility. He is the God who is enough.

So when God revealed himself as El Shaddai, he wasn't simply saying he was an all-powerful God. He was wooing Abram and Sarai with a picture of a God who could and would meet their needs. He is a God who makes the barren fertile, who desires and is able to bring life and beauty and wonder where there were once only death, dryness, and despair.

In his very name he was calling them to come. Come to the One who would suffice, the One who could quench their thirst, the One who brought springs in the desert (see Isaiah 41). The One who must be enough for them *before* they can become who God created them to be.

It is the same for us. We cannot draw closer to God until we see more of who he truly is. We must see him as El Shaddai before we can become who we are meant to be, and before he can truly fulfill his promises to us. As we discover more and more of who *he* is, we become more and more who *we* really are.

After his wife died, C. S. Lewis wrote in his journal (which was later published in his book, *A Grief Observed*),

> You can't, in most things, get what you want if you want it too desperately. . . . And so, perhaps, with God. . . . The time when there is nothing at all in your soul except a cry for help may be just the time when God can't give it: you are like the drowning man who can't be helped because he clutches and grabs. Perhaps your own reiterated cries deafen you to the voice you hoped to hear. On the other hand, "Knock and it shall be opened." But does knocking mean hammering and kicking the door like a maniac?[2]

I've been there. So had Sarai. When we are desperate, when we are kicking down the door, when we'll try anything, when we give our maidservant to our husband to have a child, then our God is not enough. He is not enough for us.

But after thirteen years of watching Ishmael grow up, Sarai discovered the God who is, who must be, enough. He was enough not only to make her barren womb live again but her barren heart as well. It is God Almighty, the One who is sufficient for us, who calls us to become who he created us to be.

Releasing Ishmael

The Bible doesn't tell us specifically that Sarai finally came to a place where God was enough. It does indicate, however, that in all the years since Ishmael's birth, she never claimed him as her own. She never followed through with her plan to use Hagar's son to fill the hole in her life, to make her the mother she so desperately wanted to be. Her plan, after all, had succeeded. Hagar bore a son. Culturally, according to the Code of Hammurabi, that son should have been counted as hers. That's why she concocted the whole plan to begin with! But something had changed. Genesis 16:16 makes it clear: "Abram was 86 years old when Hagar gave birth to Ishmael *for Abram*" (emphasis mine).

By Canaanite law, Ishmael was Sarai's right. But she gave up her rights. He was her back-up plan. She abandoned her plan. He was supposed to be the answer. Instead, she consented to live with questions instead of answers and waited for God.

And God came. He revealed himself in a new way and this time included Sarai specifically in the covenant.

But lest we think we can get up the gumption, work up our will-power to make God enough so we can get what we want, we must remember that Sarai lived thirteen years with Ishmael. Thirteen years of giving up her rights, of abandoning her plans, of waiting. And even then, it was God who appeared and gave Abram and Sarai his new name. They did not force God's hand by doing everything right. They found no formula to make God act. No action to force his hand. Change, newness, and promise come solely from the hands of God, as gifts of grace.

We must wait. We must let go of Ishmael, release our own plans on how to fill the hole inside. We must live with the questions and wait for the answers if we are to become who God intends us to be.

We must wait.

And then, we must walk.

Walk Before Him

After we have waited, and after God has revealed himself to us in more intimate ways, then comes the call to a deeper relationship with him. In Genesis 17:1, directly after God says, "I am El Shaddai," he calls them to a new intimacy with him: "Walk with me and be trustworthy." Other versions read, "Walk before me faithfully and be blameless" (NIV), "Walk before me, and be thou perfect" (KJV), "Walk in my presence and be pure-hearted" (CJB). The last comes closest to the nuance of the original Hebrew. When God tells us to "walk," he means to move forward, to live our lives. So here God was calling Abram and Sarai to live in his presence fully and with all their hearts. Furthermore, when God told them to be pure-hearted, he was not calling them to be sinless. The word translated "trustworthy, blameless, perfect, pure-hearted" is the same Hebrew word used for the type of sacrifice God requires. It is a sacrifice without blemish. It means the animal is whole; it has all its parts. It's not missing a leg or an ear or an eye.

Therefore, when God called Abram (and therefore Sarai) to walk with him and be blameless, he was calling them to a wholehearted devotion to God. This is relational in nature. It's not about following rules to be perfect but about a 100 percent commitment to walking before God, in relationship with him, every day of their lives.

Only then would Sarai be ready to become Sarah.

Only then are we ready to become who God created us to be.

113

Becoming Sarah

Sarah is the only woman in the Bible whose name was changed. In Genesis 17, God appeared, gave his name, renewed the covenant, gave Abram the name of Abraham, and established the covenant sign of circumcision. It seemed as if the conversation was over. Scholar Gordon Wenham says, "At this point, one might have anticipated that the LORD would have stopped speaking. Both sides of the covenant have been explained. The natural next step would have been to report Abraham's obedience. . . . But instead God goes on talking. . . . Suddenly God announces that Sarai's name must be changed to Sarah."[3]

Genesis 17:15-16 reads, "God said to Abraham, 'As for your wife Sarai, you will no longer call her Sarai. Her name will now be Sarah. I will bless her and even give you a son from her. I will bless her so that she will become nations, and kings of peoples will come from her.'"

These words so shocked the old man that Genesis 17:17 tells us, "Abraham fell on his face and laughed. He said to himself, Can a 100-year-old man become a father, or Sarah, a 90-year-old woman, have a child?" This was unheard of. It was unthinkable. It was impossible.

It should shock us too. Not because an old woman can become pregnant through the power of God. After all, the Savior himself would be born to a virgin. But we should be stunned because God waited until the promise was impossible. He waited twenty-five years.

And then, before he gave Sarai a son, he changed her into Sarah, a new creation, a new life, a new hope. The meaning of her name was not significantly changed (both mean "princess"), but the fact that her name was changed is important. In the Bible, names often represent blessing and God's purposes/calling in one's life. They speak of character and destiny. They are personal. And here, twice God linked Sarah's renaming to "I will bless her." He would make Sarai into Sarah, into the woman, and the mother, that he intended her to be. He would not be thwarted. He called not just Abraham but also Sarah to be new.

Now, even before Isaac was born, Sarah received her true identity from God. Before she became Mom, she became Sarah. God took her worst self from the previous chapter in Genesis and created from it her true self.

He can do the same for you. But will you accept it?

Naming is not only a sign of intimacy—the one who is closest to you gives your name—it is also a sign of authority and submission. The namer has authority over the one who is named. And by accepting the new name, a person is agreeing to put herself under the authority of the namer.

Sarah received her new name. She was known as Sarah ever after. In doing so, she accepted El Shaddai as her master. She agreed to walk fully, wholeheartedly, before him all the days of her life. New fidelity. New intimacy.

She belonged to God. He was enough.

And so she became Sarah.

You Are Not Moe

Names matter. Knowing who we truly are matters. I was reminded of this truth not long ago on a Friday night at our local women's homeless shelter. My daughters and I had gone with a small group of women from our church to play and make crafts with the kids at the shelter just as we did every month. I was in charge of name tags. I love being in charge of name tags.

I slapped down a dozen blank tags in front of the kids at the shelter. "All right, everyone, step right up and tell me your name." My daughter handed me a purple pen. I motioned to a boy of about eight.

He hesitated, then came forward. "I'm John."

I wrote his name, added a smiley face, and placed the sticker carefully on his shirt.

Next came Juanita, Miguel, Michael, and Ashley.

Behind them stood a little girl with big brown eyes and two short pigtails. She stuck her fingers in her mouth.

"What's your name, princess?"

She looked at her toes. She shuffled her feet. She wiped her wet hands on her blouse.

"You know, if you don't want to tell me, I can always call you Moe."

Her gaze shot up.

"I call everyone Moe if I don't know their name."

Miguel giggled. "I wouldn't want to be Moe."

Juanita wrinkled her nose. "Me, neither."

Ashley checked her name tag and made sure it was stuck tight. "My name is Ashley."

They stuck out their chests and pointed to their name tags.

The little girl tried on a tiny smile. "I'm not Moe."

"I didn't think so."

"I'm Victoria."

"Ah, Victoria. A much better name than Moe for such a nice little girl." I wrote it on the tag, drew three hearts, and placed the tag on her shirt.

She grinned, then poked a soggy finger at my sticker-less shirt. "What's your name?"

I fake-gasped. "Oh no!"

All the kids laughed. "You're Moe!"

I chuckled and quickly wrote my name on a tag and stuck it on my shirt. "There, that's much better."

After that, with everyone properly named, we all had a great time making bead necklaces, playing with Play-Doh and plastic dinosaurs, and building little relationships right there under the fluo rescent lights and in a place no one called home.

Real relationships require someone who knows who you really are. They require your true name.

Nobody wants to be Moe (unless that's your real name). We know who we really are only when God calls us by name. We find our true names, our true selves in walking intimately with him.

In Isaiah 43:1, God says, "Don't fear, for I have redeemed you; I have called you by name; you are mine." And John 10:3 says of Jesus, "He calls his own sheep by name and leads them out."

God knows my name. Jesus calls me specifically and leads me. He calls me to walk wholeheartedly with the God who is enough.

To God, I am not Moe. I am Beloved. I am Daughter. I am Redeemed. I am Precious. He writes my name not on a paper sticker, but on my heart. So, just like Victoria, I don't need to suck on my fingers and stare at my feet. Instead, I should wear my "name tag" confidently, knowing that only in him will I find who I really am.

Because I am known by him.

Who Is This God?

Our God is the God who names. He knows who we truly are. Throughout the Bible, God gives new names to those who are called according to his purpose.

- He changed Jacob's name to Israel, a man who struggled with God and won, a man who struggled and submitted at last. (Genesis 32:17-28)
- Jesus changed Simon's name to Peter, the rock, and said, "I'll build my church on this rock." (Matthew 16:18)
- He made Levi's name Matthew. (Mark 2:14; Matthew 9:9)
- Saul's name was changed to Paul after his dramatic conversion. (Acts 13:9)

And God would choose the names of Sarah's son, Isaac, Elizabeth's son, John, and his own son, Jesus, before any of them were born.

God is a God who names. He says of those who continue to walk intimately with him, "I will also give to each of them a white stone with a new name written on it" (Revelation 2:17) and "I won't scratch out their names from the scroll of life, but will declare their names in the presence of my Father and his angels" (Revelation 3:5).

God gives you your true name. He knows it and declares it. He tells us who we are. Not our failures, not our faults, not our mess-ups, not our spouses, not our friends, not our enemies—none of these define us. We are who God says we are.

A small sampling of the names he gives:

- friend (John 15:15)
- child (1 John 3:1)
- son or daughter (2 Corinthians 6:18)
- heir (Galatians 4:7)
- saint (KJV: 1 Corinthians 1:2; Ephesians 1:1; Philippians 1:1; Colossians 1:2)
- chosen, holy, beloved (Colossians 3:12)
- holy, blameless (Ephesians 1:4)

- treasured (Deuteronomy 7:6; Psalm 135:4)
- precious (Isaiah 43:4)
- blessed (Psalm 65:4 KJV)

The question is, will we accept the name he gives us? Will we live our life as the one he calls us to be? Will we walk intimately, wholeheartedly with him every day as Sarah, not as Sarai?

I am Sarah. You are Sarah. And he is asking us for everything, for a complete commitment to relationship with him. Only then do we become our true selves, because of his grace, because of his love.

Come to El Shaddai, draw close and hear him whisper your new name.

Come and become.

> Nations will see your righteousness,
>   all kings your glory.
> You will be called by a new name,
>   which the LORD's own mouth will determine.

> —Isaiah 62:2

9

LAUGHTER AND LIES: IS ANYTHING TOO DIFFICULT FOR THE LORD?

The LORD appeared to Abraham at the oaks of Mamre.... "Where's your wife Sarah?" And he said, "Right here in the tent." Then one of the men said, "I will definitely return to you about this time next year. Then your wife Sarah will have a son!" Sarah was listening at the tent door behind him.... Sarah laughed to herself, thinking, I'm no longer able to have children and my husband's old. The LORD said to Abraham, "Why did Sarah laugh and say, 'Me give birth? At my age?' Is anything too difficult for the LORD? When I return to you about this time next year, Sarah will have a son." Sarah lied and said, "I didn't laugh," because she was frightened. But he said, "No, you laughed."

—Genesis 18:1, 9-10, 12-15

SOMETIMES YOU JUST WANT to hide. You don't want to hear the promises again because it seems too late. And it's easier to laugh in disbelief, to conclude God has turned his back. Because hope is hard. Sometimes it hurts.

But God sees us even when we hide. He hears us when we cannot even say our thoughts aloud. He knows us and speaks hope, especially when we think his back is turned.

That is our God. He is the one who looks squarely at impossibilities and whispers gently, "Is anything too difficult for the Lord?"

I long to believe him. I yearn to walk in faith, to come out from my tent and truly believe. But sometimes I laugh. And sometimes I lie.

Sometimes I'm very much like Sarah. And God stands near the tent door, offering me more than I ever dared to dream.

That is our God.

For Sarah, I imagine it may have happened like this.

Sarah Tells Her Story

I am old. I feel the years deep in my bones. I carry them like stones in my soul. I look down at wrinkled hands, once smooth. Do they shake just a little? Then I close my eyes. I don't want to see. I don't want to know. It is too hard to remember the years gone by, to feel them, to carry them and know that promises are long past.

So I wait here, wait for nothing. I wait in the heat of the day when no breeze blows through the leaves of the great oak. I wait as Abraham sits and rests, an old man at the entrance of our tent, napping in the slice of shade.

I stay inside, safe from the heat but not from the years.

We are at Mamre again. And I remember how my Abraham built an altar to the Lord here so many years ago. An eternity ago, when our God told him to look up and gaze to the north, south, east, and west. All the land he saw was to be given to our descendants, descendants who were to be like the dust of the earth.

As plentiful as dust. And still I don't even have a grain of sand. Barren. As always.

I sigh and turn from my thoughts. I listen to the last of the workers returning to their tents for their afternoon rest.

I watch the dust settle in the air. I watch it and do not weep. The time for tears is long past. I have shed too many already.

I glance out the tent flap. It is the very hottest part of the day. Cattle huddle under the shade of the oaks. A donkey swishes its tail. A camel looks out over the plain toward Sodom. A beautiful city, an evil one. And for once I am glad for the oaks of Mamre, glad to be here in the desolation.

I move deeper into the tent. I have mending to do and preparation for the evening meal. But then there is a rustle outside. Voices. Abraham's. And some I don't recognize. I go toward the tent flap. Before I can lift it, Abraham rushes through.

"Hurry! Knead three seahs of the finest flour and make some baked goods!"

"Three seahs? So much?"

"Yes, we have guests!"

"Are we entertaining an army?" I peek from the tent. "There are but three. Who are they?"

"I don't know. But they are not normal travelers. There's something . . . I don't know, but only the finest for these guests. Please, Sarah."

He runs back out. Runs! Men of his age and stature do not run. But Abraham does. And for these strange men. I know he will find our best calf and have a servant prepare it. He will add butter and milk. And I will prepare three whole seahs, enough to feast dozens, fine enough for a king.

I grab what I need. Flour and water, milk, and a touch of butter. I knead the bread, my fingers sinking deep into the dough. I knead, I bake, and I wonder.

Who are these men who have come to the great oaks of Mamre, to the place where my husband built an altar and sacrificed to our God?

I bake the bread quickly. Abraham serves it.

I will not go out. I cannot. I dare not. So I hide here in my tent, in the shadows, away from the light of day, from the eyes of men who look like travelers but could be more. I hide from them. I hide from hope.

I hear a man's voice, deep, resonant. "Where's your wife Sarah?" He calls me by my new name, my true name, this man who has not seen me.

Abraham answers, "Right here in the tent."

I peek out, just barely. The men still have their backs to me. Abraham is motioning toward me. I shake my head. I do not move. I cannot. I dare not. The shadows are my cloak. I pull them tighter around me.

Then one of the men speaks again. He speaks with authority and confidence. He speaks to my soul, and my heart breaks. "I will definitely return to you about this time next year," he states. "Then your wife Sarah will have a son!"

A laugh bubbles within me. A son? At my age? I'm no longer able to have children, and my husband's old! I glance at my wrinkled hands. They are shaking now with age and disbelief, with pain and the bitterness of too many years of disappointment. A son? The laugh threatens to spill out. I swallow it. I keep it to myself, bury it in my heart. I laugh within.

And the man speaks again. The one in the middle. "Why did Sarah laugh and say, 'Me give birth? At my age?'" He pauses, the question heavy in the air.

How did he know? I am behind him. I am hidden. The shadows are my garment. I shrink from the light. He does not see me. He cannot. Can he?

Who is this man who sees into my soul?

His next words pierce me, undo me. "Is anything too difficult for the Lord? When I return to you about this time next year, Sarah will have a son."

The Lord? The Lord is here. He sees me. He knows me. And I have laughed at the promise of El Shaddai.

Now my hands truly shake. Now I know fear. And maybe, perhaps, a hint of hope.

Words slip from my lips. The only ones I speak. Quiet words. Foolish words. "I didn't laugh." A lie.

He does not turn as he speaks again. He doesn't look, but I know he sees. I know he hears. "No, you laughed." The truth, bold and unadorned. It swallows up my lie and leaves nothing but truth, nothing but hope, in its place. No shame. No condemnation. Just the truth.

The impossible truth.

I cannot hide in shadows. I cannot hide in lies. I dare not hide from this one who sees me. I thought to serve here in the tent, unknown and uncalled.

But he has called me. He has seen me. He has heard the silent laugh of my soul. Is anything too difficult for El Shaddai?

Do I dare believe?

Do I dare hope again?

Waiting for Wonder

Hope. We think of it as a blessing, as a lifting of the heaviness of life. But sometimes the weight of it—the wait of it—is more than we can bear. Sometimes it's just too hard to hope anymore.

Sometimes we are like a bird toyed with too long by the cat. A few years ago, one of our cats, Friskey, captured a little bird. He held it in his mouth then let it go. It hopped a few inches away. Then Friskey pounced again. He held it under his paw. Again and again the cat would release the tiny bird only to capture it again. Finally, my daughters and I were able to rescue the bird from the cat's claws.

I held the tiny creature in my hand. It lay still, its heart pounding beneath my fingers.

I checked it carefully. Friskey had not harmed it. There were no bites, no pulled feathers, no blood.

But there was also no hope.

Again and again it had tried to escape from Friskey. Again and again Friskey captured it.

Now it would not even try. It could not. So I placed an old towel on the porch, put the still-immobile bird on the towel, and surrounded it with an old piece of fencing, tall enough that Friskey could not get in if he should come back.

The bird sat on the towel and did nothing but blink and breathe. Blink and breathe.

I waited, and waited, and waited.

Still the bird did not fly away. It sat there for hours, rescued, unharmed, and completely immobilized by lingering fear, by the weight of hope too often disappointed. I spoke gently to it. I fluttered my fingers at it. I left it alone. Even when Friskey returned and stared through the fence slats, it did not choose freedom.

It chose fear.

It was too hard to hope. So it hid.

It hid for most of the day until it finally fluttered out of its enclosure and settled in a distant tree. It took all those hours for it to dare to hope again.

It took Sarah a long time too.

Unhidden (Called from the Tent)

When hope came knocking in the form of three strangers, Sarah hid in the tent. She served, and she cooked bread enough for a feast. She didn't complain. She did her duty. But she stayed away. Some commentators believe that staying hidden was simply the custom for married women of the time. But we see no other biblical evidence that suggests women had to be tucked away in their tents whenever guests arrived.

Sarah *chose* the tent.

Sometimes we do too. Sometimes it's just easier to serve silently in the background, to cook, to provide, and never dream of more. We do what we're asked. We have been renamed, but the promises remain beyond us. We've been disappointed too often. And now we believe that the barren tent is all there is.

But God does not allow us to hide in the tents of our churches, our families, or our lives. He calls us, as he did Sarah, by our true names. He searches for us. He finds us, no matter how deeply we are hidden.

Abraham's visitors ate their meal, and then we expected them to deliver a message to Abraham from God. We were listening for prophecy.

Instead they made an inquiry. "Where's your wife Sarah?" Such a question was not customary. Not only did they ask after Abraham's wife, they used her name. And not her old name of Sarai, but her new, God-given name.

Only after Sarah had been unhidden, only after she'd been pointed out as "right here in the tent" did the prophecy occur. And it was said with conviction: "I will definitely return to you about this time next year. Then your wife Sarah will have a son!"

Sarah was listening at the tent door "behind him." She was still attempting to maintain a measure of hiddenness. The speaker's back was toward her. But he heard her, he saw her, he spoke to her by speaking to Abraham.

God sees us in the shadows of our tents, in the places we hide because we are afraid to hope anymore. He sees us and he speaks.

When we think his back is turned, when we believe God can't see our pain, when we fear he has forgotten us, when it seems too late: that's when he calls our names, our true names. He calls us from the tent.

And he asks us to believe again. Believe the impossible. Believe when it seems we're too old and it's too late. Against all odds, can we still believe?

Impossible Promises (Laughter)

Sarah couldn't. She laughed, incredulous at the promise of a son at her age. And she was right. It was impossible. She was old. Abraham was old. The time for childbearing was long past.

And that, apparently, was just how God wanted it. He wanted it to be impossible. He could have easily given Sarah a son years before, before menopause kicked in and ended her chances. But God didn't act while Sarah was young. He waited until the chances were not even slim to none—they were just none.

God waited until there was no way other than a miracle. The chances were gone, the conniving ended. There was nothing left but him and the last call to believe anyway, hope anyway, trust anyway.

But it was hard. So hard. And Sarah could only laugh, and even that laugh was hidden deep inside.

But her laughter of doubt didn't disqualify her from receiving what God had promised. God didn't take back the promise. Instead he repeated it. And he called her to believe, to deepen her faith, to think rationally and reasonably.

Again, he called what was hidden into the light.

God does the same for us. Our deepest doubts, our bitterest laughter, the places of dark, hopeless pain—he sees, he hears, when we protect ourselves as best we can from being disappointed again, when we say aloud that we believe but cannot live as if we do. Our God knows us in our hidden hearts where laughter is colored with the strain of the long wait. He knows us and doesn't condemn. Instead, he calls us deeper.

Is Anything Too Difficult for the Lord?

He calls us, as he called Sarah, with the quiet question, "Is anything too difficult for the Lord?" In Hebrew, the word used for "difficult" here doesn't simply mean that it will take a lot of work. Rather, it refers to something that goes beyond what human hard work can attain. No amount of human stick-to-it-ness can accomplish the goal. Basically he is saying that because he is the Lord, even that which is impossible for Sarah and Abraham (and us!) is possible for him. Even the humanly unattainable for is not too difficult for the Lord.

How different from our cultural "you can do anything you set your mind to" philosophy! You can't. You are not God.

God does not call us to believe that we can do anything if only we try hard enough. He calls us to trust him in the face of the impossible. He calls us to believe *him*, to trust *him*, instead of ourselves. Many things, not just birthing a son long after menopause, are too difficult for us. But nothing is too difficult for the Lord.

I was reminded of this again when I faced another impossible day in my normally impossible life.

I woke to Jayden's blood glucose monitor shrilly announcing low blood sugar, one twin fiercely arguing with the four-year-old about a pencil, the bunnies escaped from their cages and running rampant (and leaving little round "signs" of where they'd been) all over the room, and a ten-year-old shouting about the Warriors shirt she just had to wear to school today but of course could not find. I should have known right then it would be one of those days—a typical day in the Schalesky household. Welcome to my life. (Maybe you've had such days yourself!)

I leapt out of bed, threw on some clothes, and raced past the dirty dishes in the sink, the pile of laundry in the basket, and the multicolored blocks scattered on the stairs.

Next, I snatched up a bunny, broke up the fight, and pointed to the corner of Jayna's shirt sticking out from under the couch (how it got there, no one will ever know). Then I hollered at Jayden to check his blood sugar with the meter (turned out the monitor was registering a false low from his lying on the sensor), hurried to pack lunches while making scrambled eggs, and told everyone to get dressed quickly or we'd be late to school.

"Mom, I forgot to finish my homework. I need help with this problem."

"Mom, I was supposed to bring brownies to school today, remember?"

"Mom, I don't like pepper in my eggs."

I looked down at the peppercorn grinder in my hand. What was I thinking? What was I doing? This was absolutely, completely, 100 percent impossible.

"Mom, my monitor is alarming again."

And it was. This time, Jayden's monitor showed his blood glucose to be shooting over three hundred, and a finger poke confirmed it. A little yogurt was sending his number into the danger zone despite the exact right amount of insulin I had given him.

I walked back to my bedroom, sat on the edge of the bed, and dropped my head into my hands.

Then I heard, in the din, a quiet whisper in my soul: "Peace I leave with you. My peace I give you. I give to you not as the world gives. Don't be troubled or afraid" (John 14:27).

I didn't laugh. I cried. I sobbed, great wracking sobs, because with that one simple promise of peace, God had uncovered in me all my hidden fear about Jayden's illness and all my pain from trying to do it all, be it all, for everyone. He showed me my weakness.

He showed me his strength.

I am not God.

All of this crazy life I live, from Jayden's type 1 diabetes to getting six kids ready for school, to bunnies and laundry and lost shirts, it's all too difficult for me. Too long I've believed the cultural mantras of "You can do anything you set your mind to" and "All it takes is a little hard work." In reality, very little of my life is actually within my control.

I can't undo past mistakes. I can't control what happens to me or to my kids today. I can't cure diabetes. I can't guarantee anything in the future.

I am not God. He is God of yesterday. There's nothing in my past that can't be forgiven, nothing I've done he can't redeem. He's God of today. Whatever happens is in his hands. He's the God of how I spend this day, this hour, this minute. None of my "now" belongs to me. It's all his. And he's God of tomorrow, of my hopes and dreams, and my fears. I can leave all that in his hands.

So in the realities of this impossible life, I'm finding it's not my job to make God's promises come true. It's not my job to grasp after what I want and despair when things don't go as hoped. Instead, I just need to trust the one who promises impossible peace, the one who holds all my days in his hands. The one who asks me, "Is anything—anything!—too difficult for the Lord?"

I need to but remember: he is the God who delights in overcoming the impossible.

Truth and Lies

Jeremiah believed in that kind of God. He lived his belief. In the eighteenth year of the rule of Nebuchadnezzar, king of Babylon, the Babylonian army surrounded Jerusalem. Jeremiah was in prison for prophesying that Israel's king, as well as most of the nation, would be taken to Babylon. He knew Israel would fall. But he'd also been promised that one day the Israelites would come back home. One day, God would restore his people to their land.

In the midst of Jerusalem's fall to Babylon, God commanded Jeremiah to buy a piece of land in Anathoth (in Israel). Jeremiah bought the land, knowing that he would soon be going into exile far away from it. He said before all the witnesses of his purchase, "The LORD of heavenly forces, the God of Israel, proclaims: Take these documents—this sealed deed of purchase along with the unsealed one—and put them into a clay container so they will last a long time. The LORD of heavenly forces, the God of Israel, proclaims: Houses, fields, and vineyards will again be bought in this land" (Jeremiah 32:14-15).

Then he prayed, "LORD God, you created heaven and earth by your great power and outstretched arm; nothing is too hard for you!" (Jeremiah 32:17). It seemed impossible that Israel would ever be restored, yet Jeremiah believed it. And so it was. After seventy years in exile, the Israelites returned home.

But I'm no Jeremiah. Sometimes I'm a lot more like Sarah: I laugh and know it's wrong.

When the Lord asked Abraham, "Why did Sarah laugh and say, 'Me give birth? At my age?'" (Genesis 18:13), Sarah was caught. The secrets of her soul—the hidden doubt, the scars of disappointment, the fear of hoping again—were all revealed. And she was afraid. She had laughed at the Lord.

So she hedged, "I didn't laugh." Perhaps she could justify it. After all, she didn't laugh out loud, only to herself. Nobody should have known.

But for God, half-truth is not truth. "No, you did laugh," he stated. He didn't shame her. He did not become angry. He didn't withdraw the promise. Scholar Gordon Wenham comments that the biblical writer "wants to explain why someone who laughed at God's promise suffered so mild a rebuke."[1] God's response was not condemnation but rather an unflinching commitment to absolute truth was God's answer to Sarah's fear.

It's his answer to ours as well.

God helps us to believe the impossible promises in our lives by telling us the blunt truth. He sees inside us, knows us, and does not allow our doubts and fears to stay hidden. John Calvin wrote, "When the Lord reproves us . . . he will [assert] . . . 'It is not as you pretend!'"[2]

We must stop pretending. We must live in truth. That's what God called Sarah to, the truth. Not to somehow work up enough faith to believe, not to earn the promise through perseverance, not to put on the mask of a faithful servant when her heart was broken and her hope in shambles. In saying, "No, you did laugh," God gave Sarah what she needed to believe, to hope again. By replacing her lie with the truth, God showed her that he saw her. He saw her deepest longings, fears, doubts, and pain, and he called her to be honest. He simply called her to truth, to unhiddenness.

And that's what he calls us to also: to live in the simple truth that nothing is too difficult for the Lord. That's what makes it possible to believe the impossible.

Don't deny your laughter. Sometimes we doubt, sometimes bitterness rears its head in our hearts, sometimes it's hard to believe, sometimes we've just waited so long. Sometimes we laugh, and it is not a laugh of joy.

But God sees us. He hears the pain in our laughter and calls us to the truth. Come to the God of impossible promises come true.

Who Is This God?

Commentator Bruce Waltke writes, "God's promise of a son is so miraculous that Sarah responds not with joy but with doubt. . . . But nothing exceeds God's power (Genesis 18:14), not even virgin birth and resurrection. The word of promise characteristically falls outside of reason."[3]

Our God is the God of the impossible. He is the God of impossible promises.

This is the God who said to a virgin through the angel Gabriel, "Look! You will conceive and give birth to a son, and you will name him Jesus" (Luke 1:31), and Mary conceived a son without ever having been with a man. Jesus was born.

This is the God who provided a boatload of fish after a night when not a single one was caught (Luke 5; John 21), who calmed the storm when the disciples were certain they would drown (Mark 4), who healed a man born blind when no one had ever heard of that (John 9), who healed the incurable and drove out demons (Matthew 8; Luke 17), who raised the dead (Mark 5; Luke 7; John 11).

This is the God who promised he would "suffer many things and be rejected by the elders, chief priests, and the legal experts, and be killed, and then, after three days, rise from the dead" (Mark 8:31). And he did.

He rose! He rose from the dead to defeat death. He rose so that every other impossible promise could come true. He rose and now nothing else can ever be impossible. Now we can live in these impossible promises:

- I myself will be with you every day until the end of this present age. (Matthew 28:20)
- I will never leave you or abandon you. (Hebrews 13:5)
- The one who started a good work in you will stay with you to complete the job by the day of Christ Jesus. (Philippians 1:6)
- My yoke is easy to bear, and my burden is light. (Matthew 11:30)

- Whoever drinks from the water that I will give will never be thirsty again. The water that I give will become in those who drink it a spring of water that bubbles up into eternal life. (John 4:14)
- Ask, and you will receive. Search, and you will find. Knock, and the door will be opened to you. (Matthew 7:7)
- When I go to prepare a place for you, I will return and take you to be with me so that where I am you will be too. (John 14:3)
- And all who have left houses, brothers, sisters, father, mother, children, or farms because of my name will receive one hundred times more and will inherit eternal life. (Matthew 19:29)
- God is faithful. He won't allow you to be tempted beyond your abilities. Instead, with the temptation, God will also supply a way out so that you will be able to endure it. (1 Corinthians 10:13)
- I assure you, whoever believes has eternal life. (John 6:47)

And so many, many more.

Go ahead and laugh. It's OK. But it's even better to step out of your tent and go to him with your doubts, your discouragement, your fear of being disappointed yet again.

Come, and believe this God of the impossible.

> *Jesus looked at them carefully and said, "It's impossible for human beings. But all things are possible for God."*
>
> —Matthew 19:26

10

NOT AGAIN! SARAH AND ABIMELECH

Abraham traveled from there toward the land of the arid southern plain, and he settled as an immigrant in Gerar, between Kadesh and Shur. Abraham said of his wife Sarah, "She's my sister." So King Abimelech of Gerar took her into his household. . . . To Sarah, [Abimelech] said, "I've given your brother one thousand pieces of silver. It means that neither you nor anyone with you has done anything wrong. Everything has been set right."

—Genesis 20:1-2, 16

NEXT WE COME TO A STRANGE interlude in Sarah's journey. After the promise of a son within a year, we might expect to go directly to the birth of Isaac. Instead we find Abraham and Sarah on the move again, caught once more in the "She's my sister" lie that Abraham used before. "This is an astonishing episode," says Gordon Wenham.[1] Astonishing indeed! How will Sarah get pregnant if she's pretending to be Abraham's sister? Why is it that sometimes when we're on the verge of receiving what God has for us, fear gets in our way? Why is it that when we're so close, "the way we've always done it" steps in to block us?

Sarah experienced those very obstacles in the incident with Abimelech. I imagine it happened like this.

Sarah Tells Her Story

A year. The Lord's messenger said a year and I would hold my son in my arms. An impossible promise, but a promise all the same. So, what have we done to receive it? Have we felled an oak in Mamre to build a crib for our child to lay his head? Have we settled in, prepared for the promised babe?

No.

Instead, we have seen Sodom fall, and we have picked up and traveled toward the land of the arid southern plain. We moved to Gerar. Gerar! Where Abimelech is king and where once more I have to say, "He's my brother." And Abraham claims, "She's my sister." Did we learn nothing in Egypt? This time there is no famine to drive us from our place of settlement. And this time there is no talk of my beauty. Age has taken care of that.

But still we perpetrate the ruse.

I am so tired of the lie. El Shaddai promised a son. But I cannot become with child if my husband and I are pretending to be brother and sister. I thought I was done with pretending.

But this is what we've always done since we left our father's household. In every new place we visit, Abraham says to me,

"This is the loyalty I expect from you: in each place we visit, tell them, 'He is my brother.'" He is afraid. That is why he makes me say it. That is why we must pretend. This brave husband of mine who rode boldly to rescue his nephew from a strong enemy, the one who argued with El Shaddai himself about the fate of Sodom, the one who left the comforts of Ur behind without a backward glance because he trusted the word of his God: this is the man who tells me he is afraid he will be killed because of me.

And so we pretend. Again.

And the servants of the king come. They take me into the household of Abimelech the king. They take me to be another man's wife.

Of course they do. I knew they would. An alliance with Abraham is desirable. And there's no better way to form such an alliance than to take his sister for a wife.

His sister.

So again I sit in the darkness and wait to see if a king will come to my bedchamber. Again I hear the rustle of silk. Again I watch the faint flicker of candlelight. Again, I do not sleep.

The morning comes anyway. And with it, a servant at my door. It is early, barely light. He takes me to the king. And I see Abraham.

King Abimelech glances at me and then pins my husband with a glare. "What have you done to us?" he demands. "What sin did I commit against you that you have brought this terrible sin to me and my kingdom, by doing to me something that simply isn't done?"

We were supposed to be a blessing to the nations, and here we are in Gerar, a small piece of those "nations," and all we are is a curse. None of Abimelech's childbearing women have conceived since our arrival. We are not a blessing. We cannot bless when we live a lie.

Abimelech shakes his head. "What were you thinking when you did this thing?"

What were we thinking? We were not thinking. We were not trusting. We were not believing the God who had promised a son in a year. We were doing what we always do. We were acting on an old fear.

Abraham swallows. His gaze skitters down, away.

Is he ashamed? I am. I feel somehow diminished. Abraham's words do nothing to honor me. "I thought to myself, No one reveres God here and they will kill me to get my wife," he says. Then he offers a truth that is not a truth. It is not the type of truth our God accepts. It is no different from denying a laugh because it happens only inside the heart. He says, "She is, truthfully, my sister—my father's daughter but not my mother's daughter—and she's now my wife."

I am weary of the deception. It is only truth that frees us from our fears. I've learned that. I learned it from the lips of El Shaddai himself. I learned it as his back was turned to me, yet he saw into my soul.

Abimelech motions with one hand. "Take your wife. My land is here available to you. Live wherever you wish." Then he looks at me. His expression softens. "I've given your brother one thousand pieces of silver. It means that neither you nor anyone with you has done anything wrong. Everything has been set right."

One thousand pieces of silver? Why, fifty is the normal bride price! This is enough for twenty brides! Somehow, some way, our God has absolved our sin. The words come from Abimelech, but the truth of them comes from El Shaddai. He has honored me with a thousand shekels of silver. He has declared everything set right.

We leave the presence of Abimelech, and Abraham prays to our God. Later I hear that Abimelech, his wife, and his women servants have been restored to health. They are able to have children again.

El Shaddai, the one who has kept me from having children for all these years, restored fertility to the household of Gerar's king.

Will he do the same for me?

Waiting for Wonder

I come to this part of Sarah's story and I am ready for the birth of Isaac. I'm ready for the long wait to be over and God's promises to be fulfilled. I'm ready to rejoice and laugh and say, "See! God's done just what he said!"

But that's not what happens. Not yet, anyway. God's promises are still to be fulfilled, and instead of rejoicing, laughing, and making happy declarations, we must instead revisit an old sin, an old lie.

Ugh.

Not again.

Off we go to Gerar, leaving the place where Sarah received her promise for the first time from the very lips of God. They picked up, they moved, and Abraham was caught in the sister lie again. This time, Sarah was taken by Abimelech, the king of Gerar. And again, God had to intervene.

As in the earlier incident with Pharaoh, Sarah was taken into the household of a powerful ruler of the land with the intention of her becoming another of his wives. Again, God afflicted the ruler's household with a health problem. And again, the king returned Sarah with a rebuke to Abraham—"What have you done to me?"— along with the giving of gifts. In both cases, Abraham's fear was unfounded. He would not have been killed for his wife, but he chose to protect himself anyway through an act of deceit. Both times, the king he assumed was godless acted righteously while Abraham's actions brought a curse to the whole household of the one he deceived.

Abraham believed Gerar was a godless place, yet he moved there anyway. And in his fear, he perpetuated a deception that resulted in the king receiving the dire consequences of Abraham's unintentional sin. Taking another man's wife, adultery, was a grave offense in the culture of Canaan and was against the law of their gods. So God went to Abimelech in a dream (a common and accepted method by which God communicated in Abraham's time) and told the king that his life was forfeit unless he released Abraham's wife. Poor Abimelech! He didn't know. Abraham and Sarah had lied to him. But God protected him, kept him from taking Sarah to his bed. We see Abimelech's desire to do right, God's assurance that he himself has kept the king from sin, and the writer's repeated assertions that Sarah was not touched during the incident (see Genesis 20).

If the nations were to be blessed through Abraham and Sarah, they had first to confront this perpetual deception and finally leave it behind. They had to let go of fear and the deceitful measures they had taken to protect themselves.

Sometimes we must go back in order to go forward. We must face the sin, the lies we live, those in ourselves and in the people closest to us. We cannot receive the fulfillment of promises to bless the world when we are steeped in old fear, old deceptions, old sins.

Fear and the Way We've Always Done It

There are five words that trouble me deeply in this story of deception and lies. Those words are not what God said to Abimelech, "Everyone with you will die!" or even Abimelech's charge to Abraham, "What have you done to us?" Instead it's a tiny phrase that Abraham slipped into his long excuse. He said, "in each place we visit." In every place they have gone to, Abraham has expected Sarah to put herself and those around her in peril by saying, "He is my brother." Even after the incident with Pharaoh! Abraham's fear of being killed because of Sarah continued despite

God's previous intervention, the revelation of the name of El Shaddai, Abraham and Sarah's new names, El Shaddai's definite and repeated confirmations of the covenant, and the explicit detail that the promised son would come to him through Sarah.

Fear: it will do that to us sometimes. It will create deception-filled patterns of protection that reject both reason and righteousness. Patterns that become so ingrained that we don't even recognize them as wrong. They are simply the way we've always done things. Sometimes they are patterns birthed from our own fears; sometimes they come from the fears of those close to us.

Either way, they keep us from the promise. God said that Isaac would be Abraham and Sarah's biological son. And that could not happen if Sarah was pretending to be his sister. Abraham's old patterns did not protect him from the death he feared but from the fulfillment of the promise they hoped for. The fear and lies only protected him and Sarah from becoming who God intended and created them to be.

It is the same for us. We must face our old fears. We must break our old patterns. We must hear a king say to us, "Everything has been set right."

The God Who Sets It Right

And therein lies the rub. Sarah didn't set things right. She didn't confront and overcome the old pattern of deception. She didn't have the power. Nowhere does the biblical account allude that Sarah shared Abraham's fears or wanted to claim, "He's my brother." It does say that out of obedience and loyalty to her husband, she did what he asked. Abraham expected her to lie as a show of loyalty. She was caught in her own fears.

In the dream, Abimelech reminded God, "Didn't she say herself ..." indicating that if she had just been brave enough to tell the truth, the king would have listened and released her. God had just called her to the truth in the previous chapter. He had confronted her lie of "I didn't laugh" with the bold and brazen truth: "Yes, you did laugh."

But here at the first test she chose to back the lie of the one she loved instead of risking the truth, the truth that would quite literally set her free.

Fear is a poor decision-maker.

But then God did something unexpected. He not only freed her, he also honored her and set everything right. And he did it through a pagan king, through the very one Abraham assumed was a godless threat.

God brought grace and redemption through someone from whom they least expected it to come. Abimelech not only returned Sarah, but he said directly to her, "I've given your brother one thousand pieces of silver. It means that neither you nor anyone with you has done anything wrong. Everything has been set right" (Genesis 20:16). The king honored Sarah by paying twenty times the normal bride price for a single night in which he did not touch her at all but rather had an encounter with the living God. He called her (and Abraham as well) blameless and declared that everything was all right. Through the intervention and will of God, the deception was washed away.

Sarah and Abraham were not only blessed with silver (as well as flocks, cattle, and servants) but also set free from fear and the old pattern of lies that was born of it.

Only now was Sarah ready to become the mother of Isaac, the mother of a nation, a blessing to the whole world.

Sometimes when God is saying to us, "Almost, but not yet, not quite yet," he is not simply extending our pain. Instead he is cleansing us. He is setting us free from patterns, entanglements, and sins we don't even see to help us become who we are meant to be.

Letting Go of "Everyone Else"

And that seems to wrap up the Abimelech story. Except it doesn't. Not quite. A strange thing happens at the very end. We discover that God has closed all the wombs of Abimelech's wives and female servants. Sarah used the same expression in Genesis 16:2 when she said, "The LORD has kept me from giving birth, so go to my servant."

Abraham then prayed and Abimelech's household was healed. The women were able to have children again. So Sarah saw the wombs of everyone else opened as hers remained closed. She saw her deepest longing fulfilled for others before she saw it for herself.

I wonder if that hurt. I wonder if she closed her eyes and turned her head while her heart silently cried, What about me? I wonder at the pain of watching her husband's prayers come to fruition for everyone else while they didn't bear fruit for her.

While God still asked her to wait.

I wonder how difficult it was to let go of "everyone else" before she could receive what God had just for her. Sarah needed to. So do we.

I remember that feeling. I remember holding a tiny baby in my arms during a ten-year journey of infertility. The baby was not mine. Even after all those years. Even after a stranger, who did not know I was infertile, told me at a writer's conference that God would give me a child, even after I heard a whisper of confirmation from God himself. Even after I'd gone through treatments that should have worked and I'd just received yet another call from the doctor's office saying the pregnancy test was negative. I held that fifth child of a friend and tasted the bittersweetness of holding a baby who was not my own.

It was beautiful. Life is beautiful.

It was terrible. Barrenness hurts.

And for a moment, I felt as if God were rubbing my face in the pain. The longing, the unfairness, the pitiful cry of why not me? I swallowed them all, knowing that God had the power to end my wait. Knowing that once again, he had not.

Instead, he was saying, "Forget everyone else. Don't compare my blessings. You must wait. Just a little longer."

Just a little longer.

Who Is This God?

Who is this God who takes us on a crazy journey to Gerar when the promise is so close we can almost taste it? Who is he who blesses others while telling us we still must wait?

He is the God of just a little longer.

He is the God of more.

He is the God who loves us enough to make us wait longer to give us more.

I ponder this strange dichotomy as I think of my life, and Sarah's, and the story of Lazarus in John 11. Jesus' good friends from Bethany, Mary and Martha, sent him word saying, "Lord, the one whom you love is ill" (John 11:3). Jesus received their message in plenty of time. Plus he'd already shown that he could heal from a distance, with just a word. But he didn't say that word. And he didn't start for Bethany. Instead, John tells us, "Jesus loved Martha, her sister, and Lazarus. When he heard that Lazarus was ill, he stayed where he was" (John 11:5-6). He stayed for two whole days. He stayed long enough for Lazarus to die without him.

What?

Jesus loved them, so he waited? He waited so that Lazarus died?

That doesn't seem like love. Yet it is.

We, of course, know the rest of the story. Jesus returned to the sisters when Lazarus was in the grave. The one who was both their friend and the God of all the universe wept with Mary and showed Martha a deeper understanding of resurrection. And he showed them himself in a way they had never seen before. He told them, "I am the resurrection and the life" and revealed what that meant by raising Lazarus from the dead (John 11:25).

He made them wait. He gave them more.

They wanted healing. He gave them life.

He loved them, so he waited.

He loves us, and so he waits, just a little longer. And in waiting, he gives us more. Because in the wait, God is not cruel but is working. He is preparing us for the promise. He is freeing us, and he is freeing the ones we love. He waits that we may be set free.

So when God asks us to still wait when it seems the consequences are grave, when he says "Not yet, not quite yet," when he takes us on a trip to Gerar, we must remember the power of resurrection, of new life. We must remember that he waits because he loves us.

He is the God of more than we prayed for, more than we hoped, more than we even knew we needed.

Wait for the God of more.

> *If the Lord Jehovah makes us wait, let us do so with our whole hearts; for blessed are all they that wait for Him. He is worth waiting for. The waiting itself is beneficial to us: it tries faith, exercises patience, trains submission, and endears the blessing when it comes.*

> —Charles Spurgeon,
> *The Treasury of David*

11

HAVING THE LAST LAUGH: THE BIRTH OF ISAAC

The LORD was attentive to Sarah just as he had said, and the LORD carried out just what he had promised her. She became pregnant and gave birth to a son for Abraham when he was old, at the very time God had told him. Abraham named his son—the one Sarah bore him—Isaac.... Sarah said, "God has given me laughter. Everyone who hears about it will laugh with me."

—Genesis 21:1-3, 6

AT LONG LAST, SARAH had the last laugh . . . or perhaps God did. I think about Sarah's long wait for a son. I ponder and smile. It lasted over a quarter century. Decades of hoping and waiting, of failing and falling, of barren bellies and promises that seemed never to come true.

Except they did. They did when all hope seemed so long past.

And I wonder, why did it have to take so long?

My heart aches for a woman who grew old in the waiting.

And then something happened. Something new and different. Something so wondrous that it took my breath away.

It is not that a son was born. It is that they named him Isaac. They named him Laughter.

The point of waiting is not discouragement, despair, or a hardening of one's heart. The purpose of waiting is to birth laughter, to embrace joy.

How could this be? Waiting is hard. It hurts. Nobody likes to wait. I hate it.

And yet I draw close to this babe born to an old woman with a promise. I hear the sound of his name in my ears. It echoes through my soul.

I know then that I am wrong. The wait is not a punishment. Its purpose is not pain. It is like the tumbler that polishes a stone: It produces beauty. It brings joy.

Laughter. Joy.

So I laugh too. I laugh in the face of the long wait. Because now I know its secret. Sarah has shown me the truth. Waiting is not the monster it pretends to be. It is the vehicle of incredible joy.

For Sarah, it may have happened like this.

Sarah Tells Her Story

$\mathcal{M}$y hair is gray. My skin, wrinkled. My belly, bulging. I giggle at the dichotomy of a bulging belly on a dried-up old woman. I giggle but do not laugh. Not yet. I rest the mixing bowl on a stomach no longer flat but round and full and squirming with life. He is a busy one, this baby son of mine. He squirms and kicks and rumbles with his eagerness to come and join the world.

I know it is a boy because it has been a year since El Shaddai appeared under the oaks at Mamre. A year since I eavesdropped in a tent. A year since I laughed in disbelief at an impossible promise.

Soon I will laugh again, but not with incredulous disbelief. This time I will laugh with incredulous joy.

I have waited long.

And now. . . .

Pain ripples through my abdomen. My fingers tighten on the mixing bowl. I breathe. And wait. I am good at waiting. Minutes pass. The pain comes again. Wait. And again. I drop the bowl onto a stone.

The shepherds are out in the fields. Abraham is with them. I cry out for the birthing woman.

Another pain. I pant.

The woman appears from around the corner of a tent. "Is it time?"

"I think so."

She calls for water and helps me to the birthing tent. We enter and all is ready. Clean cloths for the baby, a knife to cut the cord, a place to lay him. I have seen it all before. But I have never been the one on the birthing bed. I have never—I shout with the pain.

Then I pant. And gasp. And pant.

Someone sends for Abraham.

Hours pass in a blur of breathing and contractions, a gush of water, and fierce pushing pain.

Then he comes, a squalling baby boy.

I hold him in my arms. He is as wrinkled as I. But I do not see the blood or the coating on the skin. I see nothing but beauty. I see nothing but the faithfulness of a God whom I once thought had waited too long.

So I laugh. Now I laugh. Fully and heartily and filled with wonder. I laugh as I hold a baby and hear his robust cry. As I hold an impossible promise come true.

The tent flap opens. I can see others waiting outside, waiting to rejoice. Abraham enters. He grins at me, a silly, foolish grin like that of a little boy who has been given his first lamb. I hand him his son. And as I do so, joy throbs through me so strong, so hard, that I can barely breathe with the abundance of it.

Abraham tucks the babe into his chest.

And now I am the one grinning foolishly. I've been with the man so many years. We've walked over deserts and through forests, traveled toward the promise and away from it. Made mistakes, been fools. Been each other's best friend and worst enemy.

But now we have come to a new place. Together. Now we have the promised son. The son through whom a nation of El Shaddai will be built, through whom the whole world will be blessed.

More impossible promises to come true. I laugh at them all. Abraham's gaze catches mine. The baby gurgles.

"We shall call him Laughter," says Abraham. "Isaac. 'He laughs.'"

I nod. "God has given me laughter. Everyone who hears about it will laugh with me."

Abraham chuckles. "Little Laughter, little Isaac."

I reach up and squeeze my husband's arm. "Who could have told Abraham that Sarah would nurse sons? But now I've given birth to a son when he was old!"

Abraham laughs. I laugh. We laugh together.

We laugh because El Shaddai has done what he promised.

We laugh because we have waited so long.

We laugh because laughter is what the long wait is meant for.

Waiting for Wonder

Just as God said. Just as he promised. At the very time he'd told them. Three times in the first two verses of Genesis 21, the biblical writer tells us of God's precision and faithfulness. He tells us that God does what he says in the timing he chooses. God is not late. Even if it seemed that way to Sarah and Abraham.

God plans everything precisely. Waiting is not a punishment. God chose the time a year previous. And in that year, Abraham told the same old lie about Sarah being his sister and she went along it with. So we know that the fulfillment of the promise was not something they earned through their behavior. We know they had not "learned their lesson" and so God rewarded them with a son. We know that they did not get what they had been hoping, longing, and praying for because they were finally good enough.

The writer of Genesis tells us, up front, by his triplet affirmation of God's sovereignty that this birth, this baby, was all God's doing. As he said, as he promised, in his timing.

God's timing. Not Abraham's. Not Sarah's.

Timing so far beyond what they had wanted or expected that they had both grown old in the wait.

At the Very Time: God at Work

God's timing is almost never our own. He almost always seems to be taking too long. But Sarah's story tells us there is purpose in the wait. It tells us God is never too late. He always acts at just the right time. "At the very time," Genesis 21:2 says. At the appointed time. At the exact time God chose. Just when God planned it, just when he said.

The birth of Isaac first calls us to trust in the appointed time. Trust that God has the details well in hand. He who can make an old woman birth a promised son knows the right time.

But what made this the appointed time? I believe God moved at this moment in their lives because he had accomplished all he needed to accomplish, not only to begin a nation but to begin it through a transformed people. Abraham and Sarah's ideas of the promise were small and narrow: a land, a son, descendants. God's plans were grand and beautiful and wondrous. God's plans included the whole world. They included you and me.

And plans like that require a miracle. They require a couple transformed to trust, not through their own efforts but through the work of God himself. God was working to accomplish his purposes in them and for the whole world, working in ways they could not see and could not imagine beforehand. And he was working not only in Abraham, the patriarch, but in Sarah as well. Through the journey, through the wait, she had been drawn more deeply into relationship with God, she'd discovered the vanity of her own schemes, she'd been freed from old patterns and lies, and she'd learned to trust El Shaddai even when she didn't get what she wanted. The hand of God had remade her, and her Father and Master had renamed her. God did that. He did it in the wait.

Sarah would not have been ready before God worked in her through the Hagar incident. Abraham was not ready before God taught him a deeper trust through Abimelech. Sarah needed the journey. They both did. And now, only now, had God made everything ready. Only then did he move. He does as he has promised in just the right time.

Isaac did not solve their problems. The baby was not the answer to their hurts and flaws, disappointments, despair. He did not make Sarah into the person she was meant to be. It is the journey that did that. It was the God of the wait. It was the God who worked in the wait.

Isaac came after.

It is often the same for us. What we have hoped for, what we long for is never God's solution to the emptiness within; it is never the answer to our "If only . . . then everything will be all right." We cannot shortcut the journey. We cannot avoid the wait. We are wrong when we think, "If only I got my act together sooner, if only I was better, if only I did this or that. . . . Then I would get what I want." No. It is God who is working, in his timing, in his way. First God heals, first he is enough, first we flounder and fail and allow him to remake us through our failings. First we are freed. First he works in the waiting.

Then the promise comes, the gift, the outpouring from his love that he always intended. Then it is the time for *hesed*. Only after we have waited well.

Hesed

Hesed. Though this word is not used specifically in this passage, the birth of Isaac is replete with God's *hesed*. We have no exact translation for it in English. It's a Hebrew word, rich with meaning and depth. Rich with wonder. Sometimes it is translated "lovingkindness," sometimes "mercy" or "grace," sometimes simply "love." But none of those capture the awe of *hesed*. All fall short.

Hesed should take your breath away.

Hesed gives a baby to an old woman when she's done nothing to deserve it. *Hesed* creates a nation to bless the whole world. *Hesed* blesses and woos and doesn't give up. *Hesed* is a God who becomes a baby born in a barn, wrapped in rags. *Hesed* stretches out its arms and dies on a Roman cross for you. And for me.

Hesed is the heart of the Bible, the heart of God.

It changes everything, forever.

It is *hesed* that brings laughter out of barrenness. Isaiah 28:28 says, "Bread grain is crushed, but the thresher doesn't thresh it forever." The threshing, the waiting, ends. You will not weep forever. Because of *hesed*, joy will come in the morning (Psalm 30:5).

Because after all, laughter is the point of the long wait. The birth of Isaac shows us that's true. Laughter is the secret waiting hides.

Laughter: The Point of Waiting

Michael Card sings, "They called him laughter, for he came after, the Father had made an impossible promise come true."[1] We wait for laughter. We wait for joy.

The birth of Isaac assures us that waiting has a point and purpose. It is not for nothing that God has us wait. God chose the name of Isaac for the babe to be born. When God told Abraham that Sarah would have a son in her old age, Abraham laughed. It was not a laugh of joy. When Sarah heard that she would bear a son in a year, she laughed too, but not from joy. It was the laugh of a woman who had grown old with waiting, a woman who could no longer find the strength to hope. She denied her laughter, but God claimed it. And then he took it and transformed it. What had been bitter laughter became the laugh of joy. Gordon Wenham says, "The context is suffused with an atmosphere of joy and wonder at God's mighty acts."[2]

A baby named Laughter. A baby born after decades of waiting. I hold those two truths in my mind. I smile. I grin. I laugh.

Because now I see: without the wait, there would not have been laughter. It is because of the wait that we laugh. God turns our bitter laugh into the laugh of joy. It turns our frantic hoping, praying, and scheming into peace and trust. And only then can we laugh at what God has done.

When God finally says "Yes!" the result is not then a sigh of relief but a laugh of joy. I must change my entire attitude toward waiting. I need not chafe and squirm and wonder what I've done wrong, and why God is punishing me, and whether perhaps he doesn't love me well enough to answer me now. I need not doubt and wallow and fear that nothing will ever change. Because the wait will not be forever, and God gives me the wait that I may also experience joy.

That is God's purpose in our waiting. He wants us to know laughter. He desires to give us new joy. He gives us a wait that we might share the last laugh with him.

Laugh with Her

But it was not only Sarah, not only the one who waited, who laughed. Sarah said, "Everyone who hears about it will laugh with me" (Genesis 21:6). This is the first glimpse, the first taste, we have of the fulfillment of the promise that Abraham and Sarah will "bless the whole world." Up until then, they'd struggled to be a blessing. They'd brought curses on the households of Pharaoh and Abimelech. Sarah certainly hadn't been a blessing to Hagar, and we've seen no evidence of her being a blessing to those in their own household. But we sense a hint of change.

Sarah laughed, and she also claimed that now others would laugh with her. A few scholars believe that she was actually saying that others would laugh at her, but this interpretation fails to take into account the atmosphere of joy and celebration surrounding Isaac's birth. It also fails to recognize the amount of ridicule and shame she carried all those years as an infertile woman. Even her maidservant, Hagar, treated her with disrespect because of her infertility. No, the name Isaac tells us that Sarah left the laughter of ridicule and bitterness behind. This was the laugh of joy, and it was to be shared with "everyone." It was to be shared with the whole world.

I am reminded of a short video I recently watched online. A tiny baby sat in his mother's lap while a person off-screen worked to place a hearing aid in the baby's ear. The baby cried and squirmed and squawked. He scrunched his eyes and opened his mouth wide. Then the hand putting in the hearing aid retreated. The baby stopped crying. His mouth closed. His eyes opened. They opened wide. And then a tiny smile crept over his face. He turned his head. He listened. And listened. And laughed. Never have I seen such wonder as on the face of that baby who was hearing well for the first time. He had cried, he had fussed, he'd been sure they were doing a bad thing to him.

But he was wrong.

The hand he thought was hurting him was actually bringing him a new, unimagined joy. It was bringing him laughter. It was bringing him wonder.

And that little baby brought joy and laughter and wonder to me too. He showed me that sometimes as I squirm and fuss at the long wait, God is putting in a hearing aid. He's putting it in so I, too, can experience a joy and wonder beyond anything I've yet imagined. So I can begin to be a blessing to the world.

Who Is This God?

I am glad that the God of waiting is also the God of laughter. I am glad he asks me to laugh with him. I am glad he turns the long wait into rejoicing, especially when it seems too late.

This is our God.

He is the God of Jairus, whose twelve-year-old daughter lay dying. Jesus delayed. The girl died. And he turned the mourners' cries to jeering laughter with the promise that death would not succeed. He turned those jeers to joy when he raised the girl from the dead. Jesus had the last laugh. And so did those who believed in him (Matthew 9; Mark 5; Luke 8).

He is the God of the widow who wept over her dead only son. Jesus turned her tears to laughter when he raised the son as well (Luke 7).

He is the God of the disciples who cried out that they were going to die in a storm at sea while Jesus slept in the back of the boat. Jesus turned their fear to wonder as he woke and calmed the storm (Mark 4).

He is the God who turned a murdering Christian-hater into the greatest Christian missionary of all time (Acts 9).

He is God when we wait for a miracle until it seems there is no hope. He is God when we cannot laugh.

He is the God of miracles. But he does not give these miracles so that everything in our lives will be perfect. Rather he gives them that we might see *hesed*. He gives them to reflect the heart of a God of laughter, a God who delights in transforming the impossible into joy.

This is the God who grows mighty oaks from tiny acorns, creates butterflies from ugly caterpillars, brought a baby boy from a dried-up old woman, a Savior from a girl who had never slept with a man, redemption for a people steeped deep in sin. He is the God who promises that wonder will come from waiting and that wheat will not be threshed forever.

We have a God who laughs. He invites us to laugh with him, laugh at the impossible, laugh at our fears, laugh at the secret of waiting revealed.

Because this is the God who gave us Isaac. This is the God who brings laughter at the appointed time.

> *Miracles are a retelling in small letters of the very same story which is written across the whole world in letters too large for some of us to see.*
>
> —C. S. Lewis,
> *God in the Dock*

12

Waiting for Wisdom: The Eviction of Ishmael

The boy grew and stopped nursing. On the day he stopped nursing, Abraham prepared a huge banquet. Sarah saw Hagar's son laughing. . . . So she said to Abraham, "Send this servant away with her son! This servant's son won't share the inheritance with my son Isaac." . . . God said to Abraham, "Don't be upset about the boy and your servant. Do everything Sarah tells you to do because your descendants will be traced through Isaac."

—Genesis 21:8-10, 12

I COME TO AN INCIDENT in Sarah's story that shocks me. Something in me cringes as I read of the banishment of Ishmael. It seems harsh, unkind, unloving. Surely Sarah was in the wrong. Surely this was more of the same jealousy we've seen before. Surely God would rebuke her.

Except she wasn't.

Except it wasn't.

Except he didn't.

And so I must accept this troubling fact: something else is happening here, something that may offend my modern sensibilities.

So I must look deeper. I must grapple with this God who sent away the older son. I must decide if I should hold to my first impressions or submit to this strange story of mocking and misery, of wisdom where I least expect it. And I wonder, if I sit with the story long enough, if I wait with the tension of its truth, will I find a new kind of wonder?

It may have happened like this.

Sarah Tells Her Story

*H*e runs toward me with arms outstretched, small feet pounding the dirt, small legs still not quite confident in their strength. "Mama!" He flings himself toward me, and I catch him in my arms. I hold him close. My boy, my son, the joy of my old age.

I kiss his cheek.

He pulls at my neckline.

I shake my head. "No more of that. Mama's milk is all gone. You're a big boy now." I squeeze him tight one more time, then set him down and tousle his hair. "Come." I hold out my hand. He takes it. Together we toddle toward the feast that Abraham has prepared to celebrate the weaning. To celebrate the life of our miracle son.

Isaac joins the children. Friends, servants, neighbors gather around. Food is passed, roasted lamb, barley bread, figs, and honey. Abraham pours wine. All feast. We laugh, we eat, we tell stories of a God for whom the impossible is possible. We look forward, and we remember.

As the meal ends, I sit to the side and allow the joy of this day to pour into my heart as fully as the wine pours into the cups of our guests. Full and overflowing.

I rejoice in what God has done. The boy will live: that is what we really celebrate on weaning day. I knew he would. So many infants die that we celebrate when a child is weaned from his mother. We say he will live now. We dare to be happy. But I have already dared. So I sit and smile and bask in the goodness of my God.

Then my smile fades.

The son of the slave woman approaches my Isaac. For a moment I think he means to play with my boy. He stoops and laughs. Not a nice laugh, not the chuckle of rejoicing in what God has done. This laugh mocks.

He sneers and teases and makes sucking sounds with his mouth. I rise from my seat. But I do not move toward them. I remember how his mother mocked me. I remember her disrespect and my anger.

But this is different. It is more than insolence, more than a servant defying her master. In his mocking, in his laughter, I hear war.

This cannot be. El Shaddai himself has said that the promises will come through Isaac. Only through Isaac. He will become God's great nation. All the families on earth will be blessed through him. That is the promise of our God.

So I know, I am sure, it is Isaac who must inherit, must receive the promise in full. But a slave woman's son has a legal right to part of Abraham's inheritance. And I see in him, as I saw in her years ago, that he will seek to be equal.

And there will be war.

The slave woman and her son must go. They must, for Isaac's sake, and for the sake of God's promise. The law of the people of Canaan, the Code of Hammurabi, says that the son of a slave woman has a legal claim on his father's property. But the laws of Lipit-Ishtar also say that a father can grant freedom to the slave woman and her children. And if he does, those children do not share in the inheritance. They trade their inheritance for their freedom. That is what must happen here.

But Abraham will not see it. He loves the boy. I must speak to him again. This time will be different. I hope.

I go to Abraham, I go with trepidation. Yet I go knowing I am right. I am right about this. But will he think it is the same as before? Will he believe I am simply jealous of a slave woman's son? I have no need for jealousy. Not anymore. I have no need for anger or scorn. El Shaddai has vindicated me. He has changed who I am.

I am praying as I approach my husband. Words tumble through my mind. *Intervene, my God. Do not let him put the boy and his mother in my hands. The decision is not mine, cannot be mine. I am different now, but I do not want to slip back, do not want the temptation. I was wrong then, but I am not wrong now. I know the boy and his mother must go. There must not be war. We must do what is right, even when it may seem wrong. Give your wisdom, El Shaddai. I trust you to protect my son, protect the promise, protect the blessing that is for all nations.*

Abraham's brow furrows as I reach him. "What is wrong?" He reads my face. After all these years, he knows my heart before I even speak.

I motion toward Hagar, and then to her son. "Send this servant away with her son! This servant's son won't share the inheritance with my son Isaac." *You know he won't. You know he can't.*

And now I read Abraham's face. He is troubled, hurt. I swallow and look away. He does not want to send the boy away. He wants him here.

His jaw tightens. "I will go to El Shaddai."

I breathe again. I have learned to trust our God. The long wait taught me that. El Shaddai will do what is right. And there is one thing I know: Abraham will obey our God. He loves his God more than he loves this son. More than he loves me, or Isaac, or anyone. He will do as his God says, no matter the cost.

This matter is in the hands of El Shaddai now. It is where it is supposed to be.

I turn away. I do not have to do anything more.

Abraham walks away. He looks out over the great plain. He waits. I wait. And in time he returns to me. His eyes barely meet mine. "I am not to be upset about the boy and your servant. I am to do everything you told me, Sarah. Our descendants will be traced through Isaac. I will send them away in the morning."

I nearly weep. I know I will appear hateful and vindictive. I will be judged. I will be misjudged. But I don't care. Because El Shaddai has spoken. And I know, he is not on my side. I am on his. And that is all that matters.

I am Sarah now. I am truly new. The long journey to this place in my life, and in my soul, has changed me. Transformed me. I know I cannot force El Shaddai to do as I wish. I know that too well now. He does not bend to my will. I bend to my will. I bend to his. I have learned that all must happen in his timing. This is his time for the boy and his mother. This is the time when El Shaddai chooses they must go. He will provide for them, as he provides for us. I will trust even them into his hands.

Perhaps, just perhaps, I have finally learned to be wise.

Waiting for Wonder

Many commentators assume that Sarah's jealousy fueled this episode at Isaac's weaning celebration. Old Testament scholar Victor P. Hamilton cites Sarah's "pettiness, or jealousy, or skullduggery."[1] Stuart Briscoe agrees, using words such as "antagonism and hostility,"[2] for Sarah's attitude. But Gordon Wenham takes another approach: "Sarah was not motivated by jealousy or pride so much as by a ruthless maternal concern for her son's future."[3]

When I read the various opinions many scholars put forth with such confidence, I realize that most commentators are not mothers. Any good mother who witnesses her toddler being harassed by a teenager will not stand by and do nothing. Yet for Sarah, even more than a maternal instinct was at work. Isaac represented the promise and covenant of God. Not only was she unwilling to sit by and see her son mocked, she would not tolerate the threat to the promise either.

For what Ishmael was doing to Isaac wasn't simply "playing together" as some translations suppose. We know this from Galatians 4:29, where Paul says that the son "conceived the normal way [Ishmael] harassed the son who was conceived by the Spirit [Isaac]." The root of the word used in the Hebrew for "harassed" is the same as the root for Isaac's name, "laugh." So most translators believe that Ishmael was mocking, taunting, or making fun of Isaac here. The word choice harkens back to the disrespect shown to Sarah by Hagar after Hagar became pregnant.

Iain M. Duguid says, "By adopting an attitude of scorn, Ishmael was declaring himself outside the promise of God. He sneered at the birth of a little baby, instead of bowing down before him, lost in wonder, love, and praise. Sarah would not tolerate such an affront to God and to the child of promise."[4]

174

Clearly something more was going on than an old woman's jealousy. We know this because when Sarah said to Abraham, "Send this servant away with her son!" (Genesis 21:10), God told Abraham to do it. And unlike the previous time when Hagar ran away with Ishmael (Genesis 16), this time God did not send her back. This time, she and her son were meant to leave.

Vive la Difference

The differences between this incident in Genesis 21 and the one in Genesis 16 reveal the wonder of what God had done in Sarah, the wonder of what waiting had accomplished.

The events of chapter 16 were born out of Sarah's despair, out of the frustration and fear and hopelessness of continued infertility. Sarah claimed that God had kept her from having children, and her actions rose not out of trust in God but out of the fear that he would never provide the promised heir through her. It was a moment of weakness rising from pain and doubt. In chapter 21, Sarah and Abraham were in the midst of a celebration of life, of God's faithfulness, of new hope. She'd said of God, "He has given me laughter." The anger and bitterness were gone.

In chapter 16, Sarah blamed Abraham for the problem of Hagar's disrespect. "This harassment is your fault!" she told him. And she cited Hagar's attitude as the problem: "When she realized she was pregnant, I lost her respect." But in chapter 21, even though Ishmael's attitude was the inciting incident, Sarah blamed no one when speaking to Abraham. She didn't even mention Ishmael's behavior. Instead, she simply stated what needed to be done: "Send this servant away with her son." Her reason was not Ishmael's treatment of her son but "this servant's son won't share the inheritance with my son Isaac." Her reasoning was the explicit promise of God to herself and Abraham. It was based on believing what God had said. It was based on faith. Sarah now fully believed God.

In chapter 16, Abraham abdicated his responsibility by putting the matter in Sarah's hands. Here, Sarah placed the responsibility for action into the hands of Abraham and ultimately God. The result is that, unlike previously, when Sarah abused Hagar so that the slave ran away, here Sarah spoke God's will and God's will was done. "Do everything Sarah tells you to do because your descendants will be traced through Isaac," said God. God's reason mirrors what Sarah said.

We may be tempted to say that God was "on Sarah's side." It is more accurate to say that, this time, Sarah was on God's side. In chapter 16, her actions were opposed to the will of God. Here finally she found herself in line with what God had planned, what God wanted for the people around her. Hagar and Ishmael were never meant to stay with Abraham and Sarah indefinitely. In chapter 16, God did not deem that it was the right time or circumstance for their departure. Now, the right time had come. Though neither Abraham nor Hagar/Ishmael yet realized it, Sarah had become a blessing to them, speaking to them the will of God in God's timing.

We see, therefore, that God worked in the long wait. Sarah was not who she had been. The difference is stark. In chapter 16, we saw a woman filled with hurt and anger; here we see one who spoke the will of God into a difficult situation and, though it may not seem like it at first, blessed those who heard.

These are the last recorded words that Sarah spoke. The next time we read of her, it will be about her death. Her final recorded words are the will of God at the right time. And God's final words of her in Genesis: "Do everything Sarah tells you to do."

Of this scene, John Calvin writes, "I yet do not doubt, both that her tongue and mind were governed by a secret impulse of the Spirit, and that this whole affair was directed by the providence of God."[5] Directed by God! That's what the long wait produced in Sarah. That is the wonder of waiting. In God's hands, the wait becomes not a stumbling block but a pathway to knowing the will of God, speaking his words, and blessing those around you with God's truth at just the right time.

For Sarah, in the wait, she gained the wisdom of knowing when.

Wisdom and the Rhythm of His Will

For me, God is never quick enough. It seems I am always running out ahead and wondering why change takes so long. I want the avalanche, the big metamorphosis that no one can miss. I want to see the landscape changed in a moment and call that "God at work." But more often, God is the God of the glacier. Sometimes change is slow, almost imperceptible. Sometimes it seems that nothing is moving at all. But glaciers change the world. Avalanches matter for a moment, glaciers for all time.

Sarah learned the wisdom of the glacier. After decades of waiting for the right time to have a son, after causing Hagar's earlier exile through her own avalanche of bitterness and anger, she was finally in line with the timing of God. Hagar and Ishmael's departure was now, and only now, best for everyone. Through it, God would eliminate, at least for Isaac's lifetime, the potentially deadly sibling rivalry between Ishmael and Isaac. Abraham would be able to commit fully to Isaac as the heir of the promise, as God intended.

And God also promised to bless Ishmael and Hagar. He told Abraham, "But I will make of your servant's son a great nation too,"

(Genesis 21:13) and later opened Hagar's eyes to see a well in the desert: "Hagar! What's wrong? Don't be afraid. . . . I will make of [Ishmael] a great nation" (Genesis 21:17-19).

The glacier changed the landscape in all of their lives, but only Sarah could see it. Only she knew what was God's will for that time.

The art of waiting allowed her, and allows us, to connect with the rhythm of his will.

Who Is This God?

Who is this God of the glacier who changes the whole landscape of our lives, who changes the whole world, when we can't see anything moving at all? Who is he who uses the long wait to teach us the rhythm of his will?

He is the God who changed water into wine. In John 2, Jesus was at a wedding in Cana when his mother approached him: "They don't have any wine." He responded, "My time hasn't come yet" (John 2:3-4). For over thirty years, Mary had waited for her son to begin to fulfill the promises the angel made to her in Luke 1. Three decades, and nothing had moved. Nothing had changed. Her son was supposed to be the long-awaited Messiah. He was supposed to pull down the powerful from their thrones, lift up the lowly, fill the hungry, and come to the aid of Israel. He was supposed to fulfill the long-ago promises God made to Abraham of a whole world blessed (see Luke 1:52-55). But so far, nothing.

Just a tiny movement of the glacier, just a simple turning of water into wine at a backwoods wedding far from Israel's capital. Just a little thing that no one but the servants, his few followers, and his mother knew about. His time had not yet come. They were not yet in sync with the rhythm of his will.

But his time would come. It would come with an arrest, a beating, a crucifixion, and an empty tomb. It would come at just the right moment in history. Paul writes, "But when the fulfillment of the time came, God sent his Son" (Galatians 4:4). Since the sin of Adam and Eve, the world had waited for a Savior. Since the promise of Abraham, Israel had waited for one through whom the whole world would be blessed.

The whole time, the glacier had been moving. And at Jesus' resurrection, at just the right moment, the glacier changed the world. Forever.

Jesus did not die on a cross in Genesis 4, just after Adam and Eve sinned. He did not come in Genesis 12 after God promised Abraham that the whole world would be blessed. He came later, much later, at the exact time God had planned, the exact time that would be best for all of us.

Through the long wait, Sarah learned the wisdom of when. Through Jesus, we learn the same. God is moving while we wait, he is teaching us the wisdom of knowing just the right time. If the Hagars in your life are still with you, if you tried to send them away but failed, wait. Watch. And let God transform you through the waiting.

The glacier is moving.

Behold, you delight in truth in the inward being,
and you teach me wisdom in the secret heart.

—Psalm 51:6 (ESV)

13

Trust in the Tent:
The Testing of Abraham

After these events, God tested Abraham and said to him, "Abraham!" Abraham answered, "I'm here." God said, "Take your son, your only son whom you love, Isaac, and go to the land of Moriah. Offer him up as an entirely burned offering there on one of the mountains that I will show you."

—Genesis 22:1-2

SARAH ISN'T EVEN MENTIONED in this scene where God tested Abraham by telling him to sacrifice their son. She spoke not a word, gave not a glimpse, made not a single appearance. She was silent. She is unseen. And her silence intrigues me.

After all their years of marriage, did she not know what was happening with her husband and her son? Could she not sense his mood, the difference between this journey to sacrifice and all the others? Perhaps we could blame her old age, but I don't think so. Not this woman. Not after all the decades she spent with her husband. She had to have known that something was not as it usually was, and that this something involved her son.

Yet we hear not a word from her as Abraham left to sacrifice her only son. We don't see an objection, a question, a doubt. I struggle to wrap my mind around that, around this woman who stayed behind in the tents while her husband sought to pass a test that would affect them both.

And I wonder if everything, if life itself, if the life of my child were on the line, could I wait then? Could I trust? Could I stay behind in the tents, not knowing what would happen to the ones I loved most?

For Sarah, it may have happened something like this.

Sarah Tells Her Story

El Olam, the everlasting God. The eternal one.

It is the name God gave, the name Abraham worshiped after Abimelech returned our well to us, the well his servants had seized. Abraham and Abimelech made a treaty there and called the place Beer-sheba. So my husband planted a tamarisk tree and worshiped El Olam.

The eternal God, God for all time, all situations—even this one.

At lease I hope so, pray so, believe so.

Something is wrong. I sense it. Abraham has heard from El Olam again, but this time our God's words have not brought him joy. He won't tell me what God said to him. But I see the strain in his face as the candlelight flickers on his features. I touch his cheek. "Can you tell me what he wants of you?"

He closes his eyes, turns his head until his lips brush my fingers. "Don't ask me, my love."

I blow out the candle. Darkness descends as we lie together and do not sleep. He is restless, turning, shifting, breathing the short breaths of one whose thoughts are like water in the wind.

El Olam?

Slowly the night passes. Early in the morning, he rises. I don't know if he's slept at all. I rise too. I tuck my shawl around me, and I watch him. He doesn't say a word.

I don't either. I know when to be silent. I've learned it well.

He wakes Isaac and two of our young servant men. Then he harnesses the donkey. He splits the wood for a fire, a sacrifice. I know then that he is going to worship, but this seems like no act of worship he has performed before. There is something solemn this time, and now it is my thoughts that are like wind-troubled water.

The wood is cut, the donkey loaded, but there is no lamb for the sacrifice.

The Canaanite gods sometimes require a life for the gift of fertility—

I cut off the thought. My God is El Olam.

I walk toward Abraham and the men. I walk toward my son, my only son, my laughter.

Abraham will not meet my gaze.

I kiss the warm cheek of my boy. Then I step back. He is not my boy really. He belongs to El Shaddai, to El Olam.

My hands shake as he turns from me and follows his father. The servants and the donkey go after. Abraham's shoulders are slumped, though no wood burdens his back.

They travel north, away from me. I raise my right hand to shield the rays of the rising sun. Dust billows from their sandals, from the donkey's hooves.

I watch until the donkey is but a speck in the distance, vanishing in the morning heat that shimmers like smoke off the land.

Then I return to the tent. I wait. I pray. I wonder.

I sit without words. I do not know what Abraham is doing. I don't know what God is doing. Something is happening, something entirely out of my hands. Servants call me for breakfast, but I cannot eat. I must pray. There is nothing left for me to do but pray, and wait, and deny the fear that whispers through my mind.

Isaac, your son.

The son you love.

There is no lamb.

No. I will not be afraid. Not anymore. The God who made an old woman give birth will not fail his promise now. He is faithful. I will trust him.

So I wait. I wait as the sun rises and grows dim. Once, twice, thrice, and more.

I wait for Abraham. I wait for El Olam.

I wait. And I am silent.

Waiting for Wonder

It is the not knowing that is the hardest. Waiting for the results of a biopsy, waiting for a phone call when your child does not arrive home on time, waiting for news when a loved one is at the site of a disaster.

Waiting while you can do nothing, say nothing, to change the outcome. All you can do is hope, pray, and wait some more.

That is the real test of a faithful heart. And that, I believe, was Sarah's test as well.

When this event is discussed in commentaries or sermons, the focus is nearly always on Abraham: his test, his obedience, his faith. But what about Sarah? She was there, but we don't see or hear her. But we can't dismiss her. This crucial test in the lives of Abraham and Isaac affected her, too. So I must ask, what does the silence say about who Sarah had become as a woman of faith?

She had to know something significant was happening. She had to have sensed Abraham's distress and known that God had once again spoken to him. It's likely that she did not know the exact instructions that God had given Abraham, but ritual child sacrifice was not uncommon in the Canaanite religions in Sarah's time. The Canaanites believed that the God "El" who provided fertility could also demand life back in return, even the lives of children.[1] This was a practice that God would condemn as "detestable" and cite as a reason that the Canaanites must be evicted from the promised land (and in some cases, obliterated) after the exodus of the Israelites from Egypt hundreds of years later.

So as Sarah faced the solemn departure of her husband and son, she had no assurances that everything would be all right. She could only wait and wonder.

She could only stay behind in the tents while everything and everyone that was important to her left on a trip that could change everything. But how different was this waiting in the tent from what we've seen her do before!

A New Kind of Waiting

In Genesis 18, Sarah was also in the tent. There she eavesdropped on an angel's promise of a son in a year's time. There she doubted. There she laughed. There she lied.

This waiting is different. Once again God had visited Abraham. Once again she had stayed in the tent. But this time, she didn't doubt, she didn't laugh, she didn't lie. Instead, she was silent.

Bitterness, fear, and despair gave way to a quiet waiting, even when she didn't know what was happening and everything that mattered to her was out of her control. We don't see her fretting, questioning God, questioning Abraham, throwing a fit, or demanding anything at all.

This is a new kind of waiting. A new kind of trusting born out of all God has done from the moment the promise was made until now. Sarah had learned to be quiet. She had learned to watch and wait, even when the very promise was on the line. She had learned the lesson of Habakkuk, who said, "I will take my post; I will position myself on the fortress. I will keep watch to see what the Lord says to me" (Habakkuk 2:1).

Sarah had learned to keep watch. In those moments in life when you know something is wrong but you don't know what, when the things that matter deeply are completely out of your hands, when you're tempted to doubt and fear, that is the time to stand firm, to position yourself in the tent of faith, and simply watch and wait for what the Lord will do.

It is time to trust El Olam, the Eternal One, the One who holds all of time in his hands.

Waiting in the Tent

As you wait in the tent, there are pieces you can't see. Sarah had no idea that what Abraham and Isaac were doing would reflect the sacrifice of Christ himself. She didn't know the intricate weaving of this test for Abraham with the salvation of us all. God was doing something huge and beautiful and scary. He was doing eternal work. He was being El Olam.

We see only a tiny piece; God sees that whole picture from the beginning of time until now. I think of Sarah in the tent, with her tiny piece of the knowledge—probably only that something was wrong with Abraham and that something besides the regular worship was happening with this trip north. I think of her sitting in her tent wondering, waiting, holding that little piece of knowing-but-not-knowing. And I remember back to when my daughter Joelle was but two years old.

She and I love putting puzzles together. We love seeing how they fit and what the big picture will look like in the end. That day, we were putting together a puzzle with beautiful flowers and dark tree trunks.

Joelle held a brightly colored flowered piece in her hand. She studied the piece and frowned. "Flower. Go dere." She pushed the piece into the open space along one side of the puzzle. It didn't fit. Her brows furrowed as she turned the piece sideways and tried again. Push, turn, shove, turn, stare, frown. And still the piece wouldn't slide into place.

I reached for the puzzle piece.

Joelle hid it against her chest.

Then I searched through the pile for the piece that would fit into the space on the puzzle's side. I finally found it—it was covered in shades of ugly brown without defined shape. "Here, love, try this one." I handed her the picture of the brown trunk.

She looked at the piece in my hand, then at the pretty flowers in hers. "No." She pointed at my hand. "Yucky."

I looked down at the piece. She was right. It was yucky compared to the flowers. It was dark and without form. But it was the piece she needed at this time.

The difference was that I had the whole picture in mind, the whole puzzle. She, only the piece in her hand. It took Joelle five full minutes to finally put down the flowered piece and try the one I was holding out to her.

It didn't look as though it should fit. You couldn't tell what it was just by looking. But if you put it into the whole, then a picture began to form.

There are dark, unknown pieces of our lives as well. Parts where we can't see and what we do see doesn't make sense. Scary pieces. And sometimes we have to take those dark pieces from God's hand, the pieces where we don't know what's going on. Sometimes we have to sit with them, put them into our lives, and only later see how they fit to make the picture whole, to make it beautiful.

Sometimes we must wait and watch, cling to faith, and trust in the darkness of the tent, and only later will El Olam put together the pieces into a beautiful picture that not only reflects his love but also blesses all who see it.

Because sometimes what is happening is not all about you. Sometimes God is working a miracle in someone else.

It's Not Always About You

The puzzle is not just your own story, your own picture; it's also the story of those around you. Isaac's almost-sacrifice on Mount Moriah was Abraham's test. It was something he had to do to fit into the picture of the whole salvation story. Sarah had to wait, to let God work. This time it was not her job to tell him what to do. It was not even her job to know the details of what was happening. It was her job only to wait, and pray, and trust. This was Abraham's moment to choose to place his piece in the great puzzle of faith and the salvation story. It was God's moment to place a central piece as well.

And as I grapple with that reality, I hear God saying to me, Sometimes, child, it's not about you. It's about what I am doing in someone you love. It's about the big picture. And I am reminded that I don't always have to know everything. I am not fond of that fact, but as I look at Sarah staying behind in the tent while Abraham obediently trekked to Mount Moriah to sacrifice their son, I know I too am called to something higher, something more wonder-full than simply knowing.

I am called to faith in the dark.

And I remember that while Sarah was far away, while she sat in that uncomfortable place of not knowing, God was providing a ram. God was making a way.

He was doing it while Sarah waited.

Who Is This God?

Who is this God who works in the dark, when all we can do is wait and pray? He is the God of the ram. He is the God of the cross. He is the God of the tomb.

Millennia after God provided the ram to sacrifice in Isaac's stead, he would provide a Lamb to sacrifice in our stead. We were bound for death as a sacrifice for sin. And when we could do nothing to save ourselves, God provided his son. Jesus died for you and for me. And in the darkness of the cross, in the darkness of the tomb, he provided a way. A way for us all.

While the disciples sat in the upper room, while they waited in the dark, God himself rose from the dead and defeated death for all time. The disciples were afraid, confused, and had no idea what was going on. They huddled together, weak and dejected. It looked as if all were lost. Like Sarah, they waited in a room with no ability to change a single thing.

But God changed everything. In the dark, Jesus suffered and died on the cross. In the dark, he lay in a tomb. In the dark, he rose again.

And then came the morning light.

The God who did that can speak into your darkness too. When you're waiting in the dark, waiting for a phone call or a test result, waiting for something to change. When you have no control, when you don't know what's going on with the ones you love, remember, God is providing a ram. He has provided a Lamb. He is making a way.

Wait. Trust. Believe in El Olam, who made an old woman give birth to a boy from whom would come the Savior of the world. Take your post. Position yourself in faith. Watch for what the Lord will do.

> *You also must wait patiently, strengthening your resolve,*
> *because the coming of the Lord is near.*
>
> —James 5:8

14

Waiting for Wonder:
The Legacy of Faithful Waiting

Sarah lived to be 127 years old; this was how long she lived. She died in Kiriath-arba, that is, in Hebron, in the land of Canaan; and Abraham cried out in grief and wept for Sarah.

—Genesis 23:1-2

S ARAH IS THE FIRST woman since Eve who played a major role in salvation history. She is also the only woman of the Bible whose age was given at her death. One hundred twenty-seven years. I believe the biblical writer tells us her age to emphasize the length of her waiting. Sarah's life was about the long wait, it was about how God broke her and remade her through the years of frustration and fear, fury and faith.

One hundred and twenty-seven years to refine a woman. Sixty-two years since she'd left Haran with Abraham. And in that time, she suffered infertility until she was ninety years old. She was twice captured by a foreign king because of her husband's lack of faith, at least twice endured the disrespect of her servant and servant's son, and once waited silently in the tent as her husband took her only son to die. It was a long road, a hard one, and yet it was filled with the promises and faithfulness of her God. It was a journey of knowing God more intimately, of gaining a new name, and of becoming the woman she was meant to be: the mother of God's people, Israel. It was a long life, a hard life, a good life.

A life of waiting, a life of becoming.

A life that would bless the whole world, for all time.

A life worth living because it was lived in the presence of God.

I want to live as Sarah did. I want to walk intimately with her God. And perhaps in doing so, I will learn the wonder of the wait.

Abraham Tells The Story

I have lost my love, the wife of my youth. We were married well over a century. And she died here, in the heart of the promised land. It is customary to mourn, but this pain I feel, these tears I weep, they are something deeper, something more. I hold her in my arms and sob. My heart is torn asunder.

Sarah. . . . Sarah. . . .

El Shaddai. . . . El Olam. . . .

I brush back her hair, feel the coldness of her skin. She is gone now. I hold only a shell. I am alone.

Together we came from Ur, together we traveled to the promised land, together we failed, together we grew in faith. When El Shaddai renamed us, claimed us as his own, we did it together. And we birthed a son of promise together. That was thirty-seven years ago.

I do not know how I will walk this land without her. I do not know what it feels like to follow our God on my own. He told me that the whole world will be blessed through our son, through Isaac. But it is through my Sarah that the whole world is blessed.

Isaac is only part of her legacy, a son is only a portion of what she gave to the world. The fullness of her legacy is found in her faith. It is found in the decades we waited and struggled and clung to the promise of El Shaddai, of El Olam. We clung to the word of a God who revealed himself to us as much in our defeats as in our victories.

My Sarah was a woman who knew how to wait. She knew how to trust. I see now why the promise had to come through her, not through a slave girl.

God chose Sarah.

I must bury her here, in the heart of the land God promised us. I am still an alien, a stranger, but it is right that my first purchase will be for her burial plot. She believed God's promises. She helped me believe. And her descendants will claim this very land as their own. It is good that the first bit of land that my people will own will be for her. Out of her life, out of her faith, out of her seed will come the blessing for the whole earth forever.

So I leave here to find the Hittites who own this land. I will negotiate for the cave in Machpelah, at the edge of the field owned by Ephron, Zohar's son. I will buy it, my first piece of the promised land. And it will be for her tomb. I will bury my bride.

But her legacy of faith will live forever.

Waiting for Wonder

Legacy is born in the waiting. A life that matters is built not through a big bang of success, but through God's work in the long wait. It was true for Sarah. It is true for us. God is working in our waiting to create a masterpiece, to create a life that points to the wonder of his majesty and love.

Hebrews 11:11 says, "By faith even Sarah received the ability to have a child, though she herself was barren and past the age for having children, because she believed that the one who promised was faithful." Her faith in the wait, our faith in the wait, matters. It is not getting what we want that testifies to the wonder of God, it is holding to faith even when we don't. It is believing the One who gives us his love, who promises us his salvation for both now and forever . . . even when it seems as though his love is a myth and his promises naught but lies. Even when there's no evidence that his promises will ever come true. That is the legacy of Sarah.

Through Isaiah 51:2 God tells us, "Look to Abraham your ancestor, and to Sarah, who gave you birth. They were alone when I called them, but I blessed them and made them many." They had no hope for children. Sarah was long past the time of childbearing, long past the age of blessing from God. Yet God, through Isaiah, calls us to look to Abraham, and look to Sarah, and find there a beacon of his faithfulness. To find hope. That is the legacy of Sarah.

Galatians 4:31 says, "Brothers and sisters, we aren't the slave woman's children, but we are the free woman's children." We are the descendants of Sarah. We inherit her legacy of faith, of grace, of a God who works miracles so that the whole world will be blessed through us. As Sarah's children, we are free. That is the legacy of Sarah.

First Peter 3:6 tells us, "Sarah accepted Abraham's authority when she called him master. You have become her children when you do good and don't respond to threats with fear." No more fear. It was killed in the waiting. We now have the freedom to do what is right and good. That was born in the waiting too. Nothing can harm us now. We need not be afraid of threats and circumstances. Perfect love drives out fear (1 John 4:18). That is the legacy of Sarah.

Millennia have passed since Sarah's death. Peoples have come and gone, wars have been fought, nations built and lost again. Yet through all those ages, through all that time, she is not forgotten. She remains a beacon of faith for us all.

I want my life to be like hers. I want it to matter. I want it to give hope to those who come years, decades, millennia after me. But legacy is born in the waiting. It is built through God's work in the wait. Sarah has taught me that. Her life shows me that God is most at work when I see him the least.

And he calls me to be faithful. He calls me to believe. He is calling you too.

Who You Really Are

The person he created you to be is made in the times of waiting. And the result is the blessing of the whole world. In the long, hard wait God is making you into who you must be to make a lasting difference.

Those who commit to God, who give their lives to their Master as Sarah did when she accepted her new name, become the women and men God intends. As they follow him through ups and downs, through failures, sin, miracles, troubles, and betrayal, God transforms them.

He is faithful. He is at work when nothing seems to be happening at all. It is then that he is working his miracles in us, around us, and in the kingdom itself.

We become who we really are in the wait. And who we are matters.

A Life in His Hands

I've seen it firsthand. I've seen it while sitting on a couch next to a friend dying of ALS. I've seen it in hands, once nimble, trembling as they barely pecked a computer's keyboard. I've heard it in speech, once clear, once sure, now slurred and halting. I've witnessed the truth, the beauty, of a woman who knows how to wait, a woman who changes her world.

I hadn't seen her in over a month except across the sanctuary at church. But that day, two friends and I stopped by her house to pray with her. When I walked in the door, I saw that she was thinner than before. And her hug was weaker. But her smile was the same. And her countenance glowed.

We settled on the couch and asked how she was doing. I expected to hear about how hard it is to live with ALS, about the difficulties of not being able to tie a shoe, button a shirt, type an e-mail, or go on the long prayer walks she used to love. I'd gone on one of those walks with her and experienced the joy she once took in them. Now she could barely shuffle across the room. I knew I would cry, and I did . . . but not for the reason I'd expected.

Instead of telling us about the progression of her disease, she asked about me. She asked how was I holding up with Jayden's new diabetes diagnosis, was I finding time to draw close to God in quietness and solitude, was I able to make space for myself to renew my soul? She told me she had been praying for me. I shared and received her love. Then I received a greater blessing.

She leaned in, her voice lowered. "I'm so glad you came." She smiled. "I want to tell you what God has done." She pulled the computer onto her lap and tapped at it with one shaking finger. Pictures flashed on the screen. Sisters, nieces, relatives who had always been hostile to the love of Christ. She had been praying for them for years, decades, without even the tiniest softening of their hearts toward God. And still she prayed, and waited, and prayed some more. Year after year, decade after decade.

She pointed to a twenty-something girl on the screen. "You remember my niece? A friend of hers died, and then she heard about my disease. She's going to church now with that friend's family. She accepted Christ." Her face glowed with joy. "And that's not all. My sister is going to church with her. The sister who wouldn't even let me talk about God. When she was here visiting me because of my ALS, she asked me if we could go to church." Then she told us about others who were becoming open to God's love since her diagnosis. A runaway daughter had come home. Another sibling had been able to talk of God to their aunt. Story after story of loved ones who were opening their hearts to her because of her disease, and so were also opening their hearts to Jesus after years and years of waiting.

Through this horrific disease, God was moving in ways she'd been praying about for decades. Years of praying and waiting and seeing no movement, and now as ALS ravaged her body and threatened her life, she glowed with the joy of seeing God's work in the long wait. She was filled with a wonder that ALS could not steal.

And I wept at the sight of that wonder, the wonder of a faithful servant whose soul was formed in the waiting, a woman dying of

ALS and yet filled with such hope that even as her body failed, she glowed with the faith of one who knew she was truly loved.

And I know that the wait was where the work was done. It was in those years of prayers with no answer that she became this beautiful woman of God, a woman who would leave a legacy of love.

Not one prayer, not one cry, not one moment of all those years was wasted. God used them all. It all mattered.

And now God was using the disease that would take her life. And in the midst of it all, she had no regrets. Because when she gave her life to Christ, she meant it. She still does.

That's Sarah's kind of faith. That's Sarah's kind of legacy. I am blessed to have seen it. The whole world is blessed.

That is a life that has waited well. That is a life that changes the world, that blesses the world.

And I am amazed.

Who Is This God?

I stand in awe of this God who works in the waiting. I stand with Sarah. I stand with the prophets who endured persecution, hardship, and even death as they waited for the Messiah to come. Of them, the writer of Hebrews says:

> Through faith they conquered kingdoms, brought about justice, realized promises, shut the mouths of lions, put out raging fires, escaped from the edge of the sword, found strength in weakness, were mighty in war, and routed foreign armies. Women received back their dead by resurrection. Others were tortured and refused to be released so they could gain a better resurrection. But others experienced public shame by being taunted and whipped; they were even put in chains and in prison. They were stoned to death, they were cut in two, and

they died by being murdered with swords. They went around wearing the skins of sheep and goats, needy, oppressed, and mistreated. The world didn't deserve them. They wandered around in deserts, mountains, caves, and holes in the ground. All these people didn't receive what was promised. (Hebrews 11:33-39)

The wait was hard. Sometimes it seemed hopeless. But they waited well. And their faith, their wait, changed the world.

I stand with the first Christians, who were persecuted, thrown in prison, sent to die in Roman arenas for their faith, all while waiting for their Lord's return. Paul wrote of himself and those with him, "We are experiencing all kinds of trouble, but we aren't crushed. We are confused, but we aren't depressed. We are harassed, but we aren't abandoned. We are knocked down, but we aren't knocked out" (2 Corinthians 4:8-9).

Their wait was hard. Sometimes it, too, seemed hopeless. They watched Stephen die, stoned to death for his faith in Jesus. They saw Saul approve of his death. They watched their friends and family murdered, martyred for believing in Christ. They were driven from their homes. They were excommunicated from the synagogue. But they waited well. As they were scattered, they spoke of the good news of Jesus. And so the truth of Christ spread "in Jerusalem, in all Judea and Samaria, and to the end of the earth" (Acts 1:8). They died still waiting for Christ's return. But through them, the message of the gospel would reach the far corners of the world. You and I would hear it. And it would change our lives, change our world, forever.

That is Sarah's legacy.

God made in the wait a life that mattered. Mattered to those she loved, mattered in the kingdom, mattered to the whole world. Sarah changed the world. Through her, the Savior came. Will he come through me too? Will he come through you? Will the world hear of the One who changes everything? Will the world be blessed? Will it be blessed because I waited, because you waited, in faith for the promises to come through?

Do not be discouraged. God is working. He is creating your legacy in the long wait. In the pain, in the doubts, in the disappointments, fears, and failures, he is calling you, Sarah is calling you, to find the wonder of waiting, to find the wonder of your God . . . that the whole world might be blessed through you.

> *All you who wait for the LORD,*
> *be strong and let your heart take courage.*

> —Psalm 31:24

A Note to the Reader

Dear Friend,

Thank you for traveling with me through the life of Sarah, who learned to wait well. As I write this, rain is pattering on my office window. Streaks of wetness tumble down the pane and soak into the ground beneath. The long-awaited California rain, after a summer of drought. Our hills turned brown. Our lawns dried up and died. We prayed for rain. We watched, we waited in the dryness as the rest of the world heard about the California drought.

But now, finally, the rain has come. The grass is growing again, turning green and lush. And I laugh with the joy of it. I laugh because we waited so long for rain.

And I know God was with us in the waiting, in the dryness, when life turned brown and the ground infertile. I think of Sarah and her years of dryness, the years when her womb was like the lawn turned to dust. But he sent her rain too. He sent life, a child, at the appointed time, just as he sent it to us. My God is the God of the wait and of the rain. He is the God of Sarah.

Now as I watch the drizzles on the pane and leave Sarah's life, I realize I am not really leaving it. It is my life. It is yours. It is a life that has learned the wonder of waiting. It is a life now filled with the hope of a whole world blessed.

So I pray for you. I pray that as you've walked with Sarah, you've embraced this God of waiting, of impossible promises come true, of perfect timing and laughter in the face of fear. And I pray that you'll find him in your own times of waiting, in your journey to the promised land. I pray that you catch your breath at the wonder of a God who works wonders in the long wait.

Waiting for Wonder,
Marlo

PS—If you'd like to know more about me or my other books, please visit my website at VividGod.com and sign up for my newsletter, or join me for thoughts on finding the wonder of God in everyday life on Twitter (www.twitter.com/MarloSchalesky) or Facebook (www.facebook.com/MarloSchalesky). I hope to hear from you!

ACKNOWLEDGMENTS

NO BOOK COMES TOGETHER without the help and sacrifice of many others besides just the author. Here are just a few who helped make *Waiting for Wonder* into the book it was meant to be:

Thanks to my giving and God-reflecting husband, Bryan, who has waited faithfully with me through all the ups and downs, frustrations, and failures of life. You have inspired me and given me hope when God's miracles were so far away and it was hard to believe in his love. Thank you, too, for taking the kids (all of them!) when I needed to seek God more deeply and write what he had for me to write. Thank you for taking the Bean all those mornings, and for reading all those first-draft chapters in the late night hours so I could move on to the next thing God had for me. I appreciate you so much!

Thanks to my kids, for letting me share parts of their journeys to illuminate Sarah's story and give clarity to the wonder of waiting in our everyday lives.

Thanks again to my pastor, Mark Simmons, for the lend of a big stack of his books and commentaries for research and for his sermon series on Abraham, which inspired me to look deeper into the life of Sarah and find the wonder of waiting in her story.

Thanks to my editors Holly Halverson and Susan Cornell who have hopefully kept me from saying anything dumb!

And thanks to the wonder-filled folks at Abingdon for capturing the vision for the book and helping me bring it to life . . . in the shortest production time that I've ever experienced (and that for a book on waiting)! What a blessing you all are!

NOTES

1. Who Are You? Identity and Shame

1. John Byron, "Infertility and the Bible 2: The Defective Wife," January 26, 2011, The Biblical World blog, accessed February 24, 2016, http://thebiblicalworld.blog spot.com/2011/01/childlessness-and-bible-2-defective.html.

2. John H. Walton, *Genesis, vol. 1 of The NIV Application Commentary* (Grand Rapids, MI: Zondervan, 2001), 389.

3. Walter Brueggemann, *Genesis, vol. 1 of Interpretation: A Bible Commentary for Teaching and Preaching* (Atlanta: John Knox, 1982), 116.

4. Kenneth A. Mathews, *Genesis 11:27-50:26, vol. 1B of The New American Commentary* (Nashville: Broadman & Holman, 2005), 101.

5. Ibid., 102.

2. Stuck In-Between: Settling in Haran

1. Aubrey Baadsgaard et al., "Human Sacrifice and Intentional Corpse Preservation in the Royal Cemetery of Ur," *Antiquity (online),* vol. 85, no. 327 (January 2011), http://journals.cambridge.org/action/displayAbstract?fromPage=online&aid=9431216. See also "Wooley, Sir Charles Leonard," The Columbia Encyclopedia online, www.encyclopedia.com/doc/1E1-WoollyC.html.

2. "Ur of the Chaldees," Biblical Training online, www.biblicaltraining.org/library/ur-chaldees.

3. Amanda Scherker, "13 Inspirational Quotes for When You're Stuck in a Rut," *Huffington Post* online, March 3, 2015, www.huffingtonpost.com/2015/03/03/inspirational-quotes_n_6786978.html

4. Holly Humphreys, "30 Quotes That Will Most Certainly Get You Out of Any Rut," Thought Catalog, May 20, 2014, http://thoughtcatalog.com/holly

-humphreys/2014/05/30-quotes-that-will-most-certainly-get-you-out-of-any
-rut/.

5. Bruce K. Waltke, *Genesis: A Commentary* (Grand Rapids, MI: Zondervan, 2001), 201.

3. Foreigners & Sojourners: Pitching Tents in the Promised Land

1. Julie Bort, "'I've Never Felt More Isolated': The Man Who Sold Minecraft to Microsoft for $2.5 Billion Reveals the Empty Side of Success," *Business Insider* online, August 29, 2015, www.businessinsider.com/minecraft-founder-feels-isolated -unhappy-2015-8; the original source is Markus Persson's actual Tweet string on August 29, 2015, from 2:48 a.m. to 3:16 a.m.

2. R. Kent Hughes, *Genesis: Beginning and Blessing* (Wheaton, IL: Crossway Books, 2004), 182.

3. C. S. Lewis, *The Problem of Pain* (San Francisco: HarperSanFrancisco, 1940, 1996), 116.

4. R. Kent Hughes, *Genesis: Beginning and Blessing* (Wheaton, IL: Crossway Books, 2004), 186.

4. Fear, Deceit, and a Promise Restored: Sarai in Egypt

1. John H. Walton, *Genesis*, vol. 1 of *The NIV Application Commentary* (Grand Rapids, MI: Zondervan, 2001), 398.

2. Bruce K. Waltke, *Genesis: A Commentary* (Grand Rapids, MI: Zondervan, 2001), 214.

3. Iain M. Duguid, *Living in the Gap Between Promise and Reality: The Gospel According to Abraham* (Phillipsburg, NJ: P&R Publishing, 1999), 23-24.

4. Kenneth A. Mathews, *Genesis 11:27-50:26*, vol. 1B of *The New American Commentary* (Nashville, TN: Broadman & Holman, 2005), 123.

5. The God Who Takes Too Long: Sarai's Desperate Plan

1. Arthur Pink, *Gleanings in Genesis*, Arthur Pink Collection Book 27 (Prisbrary Publishing, 2012), Kindle Location 3364 of 8048.

2. E. A. Speiser, *Genesis* (Garden City, NY: Doubleday, 1964), 120.

7. Becoming Your Worst You: Mistreating a Pregnant Slave

1. John H. Walton, *Genesis*, vol. 1 of *The NIV Application Commentary* (Grand Rapids, MI: Zondervan, 2001), 447.

8. Becoming Your True You: A New Name for Sarai

1. "Canaanite Religion," New World Encyclopedia, www.newworldencyclopedia
.org/entry/Canaanite_Religion.
2. C. S. Lewis, *A Grief Observed* (New York, NY: Bantam, 1976), 53–54.
3. Gordon Wenham, *Genesis 16-50*, vol. 2 of *Word Biblical Commentary* (Dallas: Word Books, 1994), 29–30.

9. Laughter and Lies: Is Anything Too Difficult for the Lord?

1. Gordon Wenham, *Genesis 16–50*, vol. 2 of Word Biblical Commentary (Dallas: Word Books, 1994), 48.
2. John Calvin, *Commentary on Genesis*, Kindle Location 5644.
3. Bruce K. Waltke, *Genesis: A Commentary* (Grand Rapids, MI: Zondervan, 2001), 271.

10. Not Again! Sarah and Abimelech

1. Gordon Wenham, *Genesis 16–50*, vol. 2 of *Word Biblical Commentary* (Dallas: Word Books, 1994), 75.

11. Having the Last Laugh: The Birth of Isaac

1. Michael Card, "They Called Him Laughter."
2. Gordon Wenham, *Genesis 16–50*, vol. 2 of *Word Biblical Commentary* (Dallas: Word Books, 1994), 81.

12. Waiting for Wisdom: The Eviction of Ishmael

1. Victor P. Hamilton, *The Book of Genesis Chapters 18-50, The New International Commentary on the Old Testament* (Grand Rapids, MI: Eerdmans, 1995), 81.
2. D. Stuart Briscoe, *Genesis, The Communicator's Commentary* (Waco: Word Books, 1987), 185.
3. Gordon Wenham, *Genesis 16–50*, vol. 2 of *Word Biblical Commentary* (Dallas: Word Books, 1994), 82.
4. Iain M. Duguid, *Living in the Gap Between Promise and Reality: The Gospel According to Abraham* (Phillipsburg, NJ: P&R Publishing, 1999), 123.
5. John Calvin, *Commentary on Genesis*, Kindle Location 6681.

13. Trust in the Tent: The Testing of Abraham

1. John H. Walton, *Genesis: The NIV Application Commentary* (Grand Rapids, MI: Zondervan, 2001), 510.